Celebrate God

Seeing Him in Everyday Things

By Gail Pelley

Prism House Media
Florida

Celebrate God: Seeing Him in Everyday Things

Published by Prism House Media
PMB 98, 2200 Kings Highway 3-L, Port Charlotte, FL 33980
www.prismhousemedia.com

The author has made every effort to insure the accuracy
of this material. Some of the names have been changed to
provide privacy for the individuals included in the stories.

Scripture quotations marked KJV are taken from the
Holy Bible, King James Version.

Scripture quotations marked CEV are taken from the Contemporary
English Version, copyright © 1995 by the American Bible Society.
Used by permission.

Scripture quotations marked The Clear Word are taken from the
book of that title, copyright © 1994 by Jack J. Blanco. Used by
permission.

Library of Congress Control Number: 2005902123

ISBN 0-9748088-2-2

First Edition

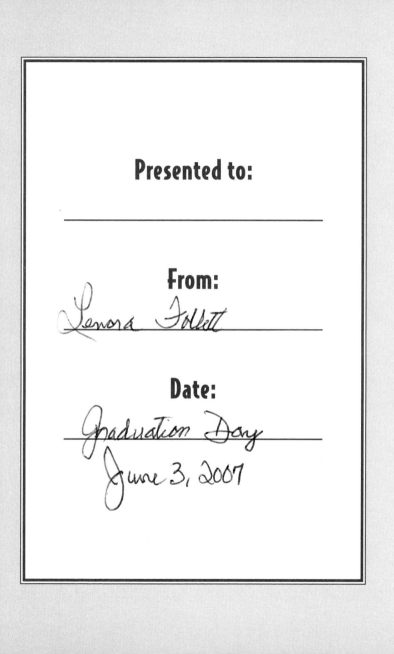

Presented to:

_____

From:

Lenora Follett

Date:

Graduation Day
June 3, 2007

Acknowledgments

I would like to express my appreciation to the people who have helped make this book a reality. They range from family and friends who the stories are about to the professionals who have helped with the arrangement of the actual book.

Katie Shaw, for her editing skills and help in making the stories flow more easily for the readers.

Toya Koch, for her work in putting the stories in manuscript form. She used her skills to format the pages, select the type styles and to create the overall appearance of the book. She can be contacted at toyshop@myactv.net.

Bill Kirstein, whose artistic abilities made the cover design just perfect for this book.

Thank you all.

Dedication

This book is written to honor and glorify God
and is dedicated to Him for His love and care
for each of us. It is also dedicated to my family
and especially my husband, Paul Pelley
and our children, Amy and Paul III,
who have made my life
full of joyful memories.

Foreword

Corrie ten Boom, in her book, "The Hiding Place," said, "Today I know that memories are the key not to the past but to the future. I know that the experiences of our lives, when we let God use them, become the mysterious and perfect preparation for the work He will give us to do."

In this heart-warming book of memories, Gail takes you with her through her stories that help to underscore the true meaning of life—loving God, and loving each other.

Jesus' favorite method of teaching was using stories. Stories stay with us, and in her stories, Gail will keep you riveted; you'll find that the two of you will be thanking God for His amazing intimacy with His children. You will probably find that this will lead you to appreciation, yes, and even worship! And our worship of Him is the greatest work we will ever do.

This is more than a collection of memories, more than nostalgia from a happy life.

Here we have some beautiful lessons from a family preparing for a future—HIS future for them and for each of us who know Him.

—Ruthie Jacobsen

The Hiding Place by Corrie ten Boom with John and Elizabeth Sherrill.
Chosen Books LLC, Chappaqua, New York.

Note to the Reader

Celebrate God

In the Bible, God is defined in 1 John 4:8 as love. This verse says, "He that loveth not knoweth not God; for God is love."

The purpose of this book is to help the reader learn to see that God is everywhere! It is also to help the reader see that God is worthy to honor with ceremonies, to extol, and to proclaim. We need to learn to look for God, also known as love, everywhere around us. Look for the love in others and in the beauty that God has created for us to enjoy.

Celebrate God! See Him in Everyday Things!

Introduction

Recently my mother passed away and the sympathy cards began arriving. Reading them was like a small glimpse into her life. One of my college roommates wrote that her main memory of Mom was being allowed to eat a tomato whole just like you would eat an apple. A small thing but she has remembered that lovingly for over 35 years. Another lady wrote of a conversation with Mom just weeks before she had a major car accident that claimed the life of her small daughter. She recounted how the conversation with Mom helped her to cope and continue on with her life. A conversation, a thoughtful act, ordinary things in the course of a life. This book is about looking back and remembering things that have happened in my life. Some small and some larger things, and God was there. Celebrate God. He is everywhere!

Table of Contents

Everyday Life Stories

Mission Stories from Vietnam

Everyday
Life Stories

Constant Care

*I*sn't it interesting how we can so often forget to turn our day over to God until something unexpected happens? Maybe some of the little aggravations that we have are nudges to remind us that God truly is with us at all times.

For example, as small children my brother, sister, and I were getting ready to color some boiled eggs. The eggs were ready and the equipment was collected, with the exception of the egg dye. For some reason it had been misplaced and, of course, nothing could be started without it. We looked all over the kitchen, in the cupboards, and everywhere we could think of. No dye. We rechecked everywhere again, and still no dye.

A project like that only holds its appeal to young children for a certain amount of time and then it all falls apart. We were closing in on the falling apart time when my sister said, "Why don't we pray?" So, the three of us got together and said a simple prayer asking for help to find the dye. After that, we searched the kitchen for the third or fourth time. There it was, right on the shelf we had all checked before! We dyed our eggs and decorated them. I remember doing that, what I don't remember is thanking God for that assistance. I hope we did!

Many years later found me flying into Bangkok, Thailand. I hailed a taxicab and rode into the city to my hotel. Having never been there before, it was so exciting to look around at all of the sights and to hear all of the sounds. I arrived at the hotel and jumped out as the driver was getting my suitcase from the trunk. I thanked him, paid him, and went into the hotel lobby as he was driving away.

At the counter, I discovered that I did not have my purse. In my excitement, I had left it in the back seat of the taxi. My money, my passport, and my return air ticket were at the mercy of the cab driver. In foreign countries it is always good to keep each of those things with you, not in your suitcase and I had been very careful to do just that. But there I was with my purse in the taxi and the taxi long gone. I remember pleading with God while I was listening to the hotel manager explain to me that I would never see those things again. He said that no one ever returned items left in a car. The drivers figured it was a bonus for them. The overwhelming feelings of loss and helplessness defy description.

I sat down in the lobby to try to sort out what to do next when a taxi pulled up to the front door. The driver, my driver, came in with the missing purse. He saw me sitting there and brought it over to me. Extremely surprised, I thanked him, gave him another tip and he then left. This whole incident left the hotel manager with his mouth hanging open, eyes wide. He said, "This just is not possible, it has never happened before!" But it was possible, it did happen, and I know why. That time I did remember to pause and thank God for His constant care.

Yet again, many more years later when our whole family was traveling in Washington, D.C., our daughter, Amy, forgot to pick up her camera as we got off of the subway. She remembered it as soon as the train pulled out, so we went in to talk with the agent. He called ahead to the next stop and asked them to look on the car where we had been sitting. They reported no camera. As we were leaving, another train pulled in and the conductor got off and asked if we had lost a camera. It was Amy's! That time we hadn't even asked for Divine help, yet it was provided. We all stopped and thanked God for his help and watchfulness.

Some small, some more critical, but all ordinary things that happen every day to someone. And God is there!

Celebrate God for His constant watchcare over us!

Stop and think.
Who can straighten things out
better than God?

Ecclesiastes 7:13 (The Clear Word)

Disappearing Act

*W*hen I was a young child our family went camping. Not for a week in a park, but as a way to reduce expenses on our vacations. We lived in Southern Florida and would go on long trips in the car. Leaving from home meant that there was at least a two-day drive before getting to the real beginning of the trip.

In order to fit as much as possible into each vacation, it was important to get a good head start. Therefore, we would leave Saturday evening and drive continuously for at least a thousand miles. My father was the only driver at that time and would pretty much crash at the end of the marathon drive. We would get a motel and spend the night, then begin our trip in earnest the following morning. From then on, we would drive until almost dark, find a place to pitch a tent, and crawl in for the night. This, along with a cooler and sandwiches, would see us through the vacation traveling. This may also be the reason that, when asked about camping now, my answer is always, "My idea of camping is at the Hilton." When we stopped, there were several chores to do: pitching the tent; and preparing food.

In the summer, one of the biggest problems with this arrangement was the bugs. One day while we were all around a picnic table preparing to eat, we were bombarded from all directions with gnats and other flying insects. Before eating, my mother asked my father to say the blessing. He was a wonderful man and a great father, but not a churchgoer. At mealtime he would recite a prayer in a rather rote manner that he had heard as a child. This particular day, at the close of his childhood prayer, he added, in jest, "and please make these bugs go away."

When we opened our eyes we were all amazed to see that there were *no* bugs to be seen. Not even one! My mother was quick to notice this and to point out the power of prayer, but my father seemed a bit dazed at the discovery. I remember sitting there in awe that God, who is in charge of the universe, was also interested in the comfort of one small family. It was the first time that I remember thinking that no matter how small and seemingly insignificant a request was, God was there to hear and care about me. And He is there for you, too! Every day, all the time.

Celebrate God for answers to simple prayers!

Whatsoever ye shall ask the
Father in my name,
he will give it you.
John 16:23 (KJV)

Thicker Than Water

On our family there were three children. My sister, Claire; my brother, Henry; and me. I was the youngest. Claire was an amazing person, very talented in art, music, scholastics, swimming, and on and on. In our house, many of the wall decorations were her pastel drawings and in church she was able to sing whatever part was needed in the choir. This was in addition to playing the piano, organ, or any of several other instruments. In high school, she was at the top of her class and led the swimming team in the butterfly stroke.

When Claire finished her sophomore year of high school, she decided that she would like to attend a boarding school to finish out her high school years. The school was about four hours from home and she had long weekend breaks every six weeks. Claire thrived in her new surroundings and became even more accomplished in multiple areas.

With Claire away at school I had, for the first time, my very own room. Of course I needed to share it with the baby grand piano that was Claire's along with a certain amount of her art supplies and instruments. Several years prior to this, I had attempted piano lessons. That was a bust because, I had no talent in that area and I was too antsy to sit and practice. The great outdoors would beckon me and I could hardly wait to get outside and play with my soccer ball.

During those years, there were people who would often ask what accomplishments I had made and compare me with Claire. One summer, she and I took accordion lessons together at one of the recreation centers in town. At the end of the lessons there was the obligatory recital in which she and I played a duet. All I remember from that fiasco was forgetting whether to go up or down for the notes and playing my accordion in the wrong direction. You can imagine the kind of "music" that made. Claire was furious. I also noted several heads just shaking with eyes rolled up. It was just another example of how I didn't measure up to the talents of my older sister. I looked up to her and was in awe of all she could do.

One day when I was thirteen, I finished my school work and went to the pick-up area outside my school expecting to see my mother. She wasn't there, but our next-door neighbor was, and she looked very upset. She wouldn't tell me what was wrong, she just said to get in the car and she would take me home. At home my mother was running around, crying, and packing a suitcase. All sorts of things went through my mind, but I was not prepared for what she told me. Earlier that morning, Claire had been on a field trip with her boarding school and she, along with three other teenage girls, had been killed in a car accident. Apparently no one was at fault; it was just a terrible accident. At age seventeen, Claire's life was over.

My mother was getting ready to join my father to go to where Claire was. Since I was the only one at home, a member of our church came over to stay with me. Just as my mother was leaving, this church member made the comment, "It's too bad that if you had to lose a daughter, it had to be Claire. She was so talented." My mother stopped in her tracks, pulled herself up to her tallest five-foot height, and said, "Don't you ever say a thing like that again! Gail is just as talented in her own way." She then gave me a kiss and left leaving me wondering just what those talents might be.

As the years have progressed, I have often looked to that verbal exchange as a pivotal time in my life. No, new evidence of talent didn't just pop up and to this day I am hard pressed to make a list of anything special that I can do. I still do not play the piano, sing, draw, or compete in swimming. However, I do understand that with that one comment, my mother did not allow that church member to get away with a statement that could have seriously affected the way I saw myself. My mother was there for me, even in a time of such personal grief.

Now, many years later, our home is filled with pastel drawings that Claire did and her name lives on with our daughter, Amy Claire. This is all a tribute to one very talented short life and to the second life that could have been altered, or in part lost, that same day were it not for my mother's love and insight.

Celebrate God for mothers' love!

Let my words and my thoughts
be pleasing to you, Lord,
because you are my mighty rock
and my protector.

Psalm 19:14 (CEV)

Waddles

*H*enry, my brother, has always had a soft spot in his heart for animals. As a little boy, he would bring home any stray animal that he found. Right before Easter he would be drawn to the little chicks in the pet store. One year, he came home with three of them in assorted colors. My mother was not enamored by all of the animals that went through our house, so Henry hid the chicks in his clubhouse in the backyard. That worked until a heavy rainstorm when the little chicks somehow got out and nearly drowned. One of them, the red dyed one, was even returned by a man who lived a block away. Henry put them in the oven at a low temperature and unbelievably, they all survived. Two of them turned out to be roosters and then the whole neighborhood was upset. The chicks had to go and they did. He gave them to a lady and while I think they became dinner for her family, I never mentioned that to Henry.

Another Easter rolled around and our mother put out the word: "No chicks." Henry listened, at least in part. That year he came home with the cutest little baby duckling. We named him Waddles and he became part of the family. He even took a vacation with us. During that trip, he traveled in an old football helmet hanging from the clothes hook in the backseat of the car. He kept the name Waddles but had to start being referred to as "her" when she began laying eggs.

Time went on and Waddles ruled the yard. At first, we were afraid that neighborhood dogs might get her, but then we watched as she chased them off. She would lower her head and part run, part fly right at them until they ran away. She did something else in the yard, too. She covered it with down and feathers until, at times, it looked like snow had fallen in our South Florida backyard.

My mother was a gardener and grew beautiful roses in that same yard. It was not a good combination, feathers and roses. She put her foot down and insisted that Waddles could not have the run of the yard. So Henry built a chicken wire pen for her to live in when we were not outside playing. Waddles was most unhappy with this arrangement and quacked nearly as loudly as the roosters had crowed the year before. Finally, Mom said that Waddles had to go. We took Waddles down to a local river and turned her loose, thinking that we could still come and play with her. This was not a good plan. Waddles had lived her whole life in our backyard and had no clue that a duck is supposed to know how to swim. She definitely couldn't swim and when she began to sink, even my mother couldn't take it and relented. Waddles came home.

Our dad traveled for his job, but when he was home, he enjoyed talking and being with Waddles, also. It was a sort of therapy for him. We noticed that if he got upset at one of us, he would go outside and talk to Waddles. He would also pick her up by her neck and let it slide through his hand until her head fell through. He was able to vent some of his frustration and she loved the help shedding her excess down.

As I said, Waddles became family. All of us loved Waddles but she never changed from being Henry's duck. If he was in the yard, she had no time for anyone else. She followed him around and was always at his side. One year, we went on vacation and a neighbor volunteered to feed her while we were gone. Later, this neighbor told us that Waddles would march around our house several times each day and quack as loudly as she could at Henry's bedroom window. She would spend her whole day looking for Henry. When we arrived home, she apparently recognized the sound of our car because she came flying out of the backyard and right into Henry's arms.

Waddles provided many memories, as well as lessons, for our family. Lessons about loyalty, devotion, and love.

Celebrate God for all of his creatures!

*I am the Lord,
and I command you to love others
as much as you love yourself.*
Leviticus 19:18 (CEV)

Dad

*W*hen I was very young, my dad used to take me for long walks on Saturday afternoons. We would walk to the beach and stop at a drugstore for a drink. I always ordered a cherry smash. While we were sitting there drinking, Dad would pull out his little spiral notebook, open it, and document: "Cherry smash for Gail—5 cents." He kept track of every penny that he spent. He also kept files on everything. After the notebook page was full, he would take it out of the book and put it in one of his files. When he passed away, I spent quite a while going through his files and could relive a lot of times we spent together, all recorded in dollars and cents. Orderly and accurate records, not unlike the records God keeps on each of us.

One of my Dad's favorite sayings was the acronym, "HWAKTMA." As a young man, he worked as a farm hand and his job was to care for the animals. My father's favorite part of the reference letter from his boss said, "He was always kind to my animals." Thus, "HWAKTMA." As a child, I had first-hand experience with his gentle, caring ways. I saw a picture of God's character in my earthly father.

He traveled during the week and would come home on Friday afternoons. As evening was approaching, I would station myself on the front steps and wait for him. Some weeks, I would be there for hours before he got home. Friends from the neighborhood would come by and want to play, but I was steadfast and wouldn't leave. Finally, the car would drive up. I remember jumping up and running to the car door for my hug and kiss.

Those times are long past, but here I am, still waiting—this time for my Heavenly Father. I pray each day that I will be faithful and not allow anything or anyone to distract my vigil. Because that first hug from those gentle arms of my Father in Heaven will be worth the wait!

Celebrate God for Dads that mirror Him!

In my Father's house are many mansions:
if it were not so, I would have told you.
I go to prepare a place for you.
And if I go and prepare
a place for you, I will come again,
and receive you unto myself;
that where I am, there ye may be also.

John 14:2-3 (KJV)

Uprooted

I am a city girl. I grew up in Ft. Lauderdale, Florida, amid houses, buildings, parks, and beaches. There were no farms in sight and no gardens other than flower gardens. This seemed like the norm to me and it wasn't until I was in college that I learned potatoes and carrots grow underground. I have been told that peanuts also grow underground, but since I have never seen that happening, it is almost impossible for me to visualize such a phenomenon. I did, however, manage to figure out how to purchase things like potatoes and carrots at the supermarket and I must have had some inkling that they didn't grow there.

When Paul and I were married, our first home was just outside of Chicago. That was not a place to appreciate farming, either. Our first home was on the third floor of an apartment building in one of the western suburbs. Next door to our building was a single-family home. Our driveway bordered that home's yard.

One day while coming home, I saw a little plant growing right beside the driveway on the edge of our neighbor's yard. It was very small but it looked like it might be a sunflower plant.

Apparently sunflowers grow slowly in the beginning of spring because it did not seem to be in any hurry to get tall and produce one of those wonderful big sunflowers. Even so, I was faithful to check on it each day.

As the spring days continued, the sunflower grew taller and taller. My husband and I discussed digging it up and putting it in a pot so that we could place it in one of our windows on the third floor. I have no idea how we thought we could grow it there, but that was our plan. We decided that we should leave it in the ground for as long as possible so it would get stronger and be able to tolerate the transplant. I was so pleased with the thought of a big beautiful sunflower in our apartment and was even presumptuous enough to wonder if our ceilings were tall enough for it to grow to it's full height.

It was almost time to purchase the pot and perform the transplant when the stalk was about two feet tall. Then one day we arrived home from work and discovered that our neighbor had done his first mowing of the spring and with it had pulled up the "weed," our sunflower plant. I was crushed. I had such great plans for that little flower and had waited expectantly for it to grow.

Too late. We waited too long before moving that plant. It was such a tender little plant and gave us such joy as it was growing. People are like that sunflower plant. They can give us joy and yet be fragile just like that plant. They can be "uprooted" so easily if we are not careful and attentive to their needs.

Celebrate God for His help in keeping us "rooted"!

There is a certain day when you're born and then comes a certain day when you die. There is a time to plant and a time to harvest what was planted.

Ecclesiastes 3:2 (The Clear Word)

April 15

*W*hen you think of April 15, do you automatically think of paying your income tax? I know that is true for a lot of people but not necessarily for me. Oh sure, I do think about taxes, but one year something very important happened on that day.

Paul and I had just purchased our very first home. It was definitely a "fixer- upper" and would require a lot of tender loving care to get it ready to move into. The home had been on the market for over a year; the man of the house had already been transferred to another state for his job while his wife stayed behind. Because she wanted to be with him, we got a good deal on the house and closed quickly. Every day after work we would hurry home and log in a few hours of hammering, nailing, and painting. After an intense year, it was finally complete.

The yard was a mess as well, but it did have two apple trees and one pear tree. The grass had long since been taken over by weeds. Each day when we pulled into our driveway we would talk about how we needed to do something with the yard. Finally the day came when we could begin to address the yard situation. First on the list was to kill the weeds. Paul bought some weed killer, connected it to the hose, and sprayed the whole yard. After he finished the spraying, we looked again at the container and discovered that we had read the directions incorrectly and had put on ten times the strength that was recommended. We were sick! We called the store and asked what to do to save our fruit trees and were told that there was nothing that could be done. It was spring and the sap had begun to flow which would draw the poison up into the trees and kill them. The man said that the only thing that could save our trees was for it to snow and stop the flow of sap.

It was April 15. Snow at that time would be very unusual. Tax day was also the deadline for everyone to have their studded snow tires off of their cars. We didn't want to be responsible for traffic jams, but did pray that God would come up with something to help us. That night we went to bed still wondering about our trees. The next morning we awoke to a white world. Snow had fallen during the night and the entire yard was covered in several inches! The news broadcaster talked about how unusual it was for there to be snow at that time of year and gave urgent requests for people to drive carefully due to the absence of snow tires.

We drove carefully to work that day smiling all the way. Our trees were saved! We were able to get some good apples and pears.

The yard was another story, we managed to kill all of the weeds as well as what little grass we had but that didn't matter, we needed to replace the grass anyway and having it dead actually made the job easier.

For a long time we heard people discussing that snowstorm and wondering how it had happened. We know at least two reasons for the snow—our fruit trees and God's desire to show us His love in a very unusual way!

Celebrate God for unexpected snow!

In my distress I called on the Lord.
I cried out to my God for help.
Far off in His Temple, He heard
my voice and listened to my cry.
Psalm 18:6 (The Clear Word)

Outdoor Entertainment

*A*my was two years old and her brother, Paul, was only three months old when we decided to take advantage of a beautiful Florida day. In the morning after breakfast, Amy and I carefully tucked Paul into the bright red Radio Flyer wagon and set out for adventure. Amazingly, it took us about three hours to go only a few blocks. I know that seems very slow, but there was a reason. As we walked along, Amy stopped to study every flower, leaf, or bug. Her favorite place was about a block from our house that was rich with wildflowers and weeds, as well as ants, spiders, and other creatures. In the middle of the block there was a fire hydrant that was painted blue and would sometimes drip water. That provided us with a little waterfall and we spent many mornings never getting past this little "park." Each nature nugget that Amy and I found had to be examined, discussed, and then shown and explained to Paul before moving on to another item. As you can imagine, that was quite time consuming even though Paul couldn't join in the conversation. He did follow Amy with his eyes though, and kept his arms and legs moving with animation.

Watching my childrens' excitement with each little piece of nature was inspirational. I asked myself: "At what age does life become so cluttered and busy that it is easy to miss all of the beautiful and interesting things around us?" "What can we do to prevent this from happening to us?"

In every part of nature there is a lesson that God has created especially for us. Whether it is to show us His order and attention to detail, His desire to surround us with beauty, or to teach us lessons about Himself, it is important that we be open to receiving these messages. Perhaps one of His biggest lessons for us is to watch our children and see how simple they keep their lives, how excited they can become over the smallest of things around them. In Romans 8:16, we are called "the children of God." Let's ask God for help to become more childlike.

Celebrate God as He helps us see the world through the eyes of a child!

Stand still, and consider the wondrous works of God.

Job 37:14 (KJV)

Lost And Found

It was a beautiful Florida morning and most of our church family had gathered at a remote beach area for our annual church breakfast. Grills were set up and most of the ladies were busily cooking pancakes, eggs, and fried potatoes. The children played in the sand and waited to eat. Finally, the food was ready and everyone ate to their heart's content. Then cleanup began. Most of the adults were sitting on lawn chairs looking at the beach, visiting, and watching the children play. As I was scouring one of the grills, the mother of Amy's best friend came and asked if Amy could walk down the beach with them. The girls were only five years old, but she assured me that she would be happy to have Amy along and would keep a close eye on her. I called Amy over and asked her to promise me that she would not go near the water. She said, "I promise, Mommy." Then they were off and I continued cleaning the grill.

About an hour and a half later, I noticed that family walking back toward our group along the shoreline. Nowhere did I see Amy. When I asked about my daughter's whereabouts, she looked around and said, "Oh, I thought she was right behind us." That was not the answer I wanted to hear.

As the word got out that Amy was missing, the entire group became tense. One lady came up to me and said, "I hope she didn't go in the water and drown." Not the most comforting thought to a mother that is struggling not to panic. I answered that I wasn't worried because Amy had promised me she would not go near the water. My main concern was that someone had taken her. I had visions of our beautiful little blond-haired, blue-eyed girl being dragged off by a stranger.

My husband, Paul headed out running down the beach as soon as we missed Amy. I stayed at the picnic site with our son in case she showed up there. We also called the police and the shore patrol. Time dragged on as the police questioned everyone and started their search.

I don't know how long it was, but it seemed like forever before we saw Paul coming back up the beach with Amy. I started to cry, ran over to her, and hugged her tightly. Paul said that he had found her way down the beach looking for shells. As he ran up to her, she looked up, smiled, and held out her hand to show him all of her pretty shells. He told her how worried we were that she was lost. Her comment was, "I wasn't lost, I knew right where I was."

I've often thought of that day. I think I had a small glimpse of how God must feel when one of His children is lost. I know He loves each of us and wants us all to find Him and the salvation He offers.

Celebrate God for being lost and then found!

Then Jesus said to His disciples,
"Let me ask you something.
If a man has a hundred sheep,
but one of them gets lost,
doesn't he leave the others at home
and personally go out
and search everywhere
to find that one lost sheep?...
That's how your heavenly Father
feels about every child of His,
whether infant or adult."

Matthew 18:12 & 14 (The Clear Word)

Delayed Gratification

*M*y husband, Paul, notices all kinds of cars and trucks. He tells me that from childhood he would always read the car magazines and dream of someday owning his favorite car, a Porsche 911. He would visualize himself behind the wheel and would daydream about how it would accelerate and corner.

One year, he found a little matchbox Porsche 911 and brought it home. He took this little model car, placed it on top of an upturned 5-gallon bucket in the middle of the garage and sprayed water on it. He then instructed our son, who was about six years old, to water it for him several times a day so that it would grow. Our son took his assignment quite seriously, even though he was pretty sure that his father was joking. I would see him before and after school with that little squeeze bottle "watering" the model car. From time to time he would ask me to check the car to see if it had grown.

That year around Christmas, my husband was on a business trip to several locations around the state of Florida. It was easy for me to keep track of where he was because each day I would receive a call from the Porsche dealer in a different city. The story was always the same: Could I please give Paul the message that the dealership was looking for the 911 he wanted. They would be able to have it delivered to their dealership in a week or so if he was really interested in buying. Then one day the call came from the Porsche dealership in Jacksonville which is at least a five-hour drive from our home and the farthest point that Paul was going on his trip. The word from that dealership was: "Tell Paul that I have found his car. It will be delivered here tomorrow and will be ready for pick-up the next day."

Not long after that call, Paul arrived home. He seemed surprised when I asked him about the Porsche. He wasn't aware that each dealership would call; however, when he got the message from the salesman in Jacksonville, he got right on the phone and made a deal for his dream car. "Why Jacksonville?" I asked him. "That is the farthest dealership from here." He answered, "I am buying from that salesman because he knew more about the car than I did. He can answer any of my questions and when I wanted to know if he could find the car for me, he said, 'absolutely, when do you want it?'" Paul had decided that if he was going to purchase the car, he would get it only from the best, the salesperson that knew the right answers.

With all of the questions these days about problems in the world, wouldn't it be great if we would question the best, check the source with all of the right answers? The

Bible is that source and it truly does have all of the answers to life's questions.

Paul flew to Jacksonville to pick up his car. When he arrived at the airport, the salesman, dressed in a tuxedo, was standing by Paul's new Porsche with the door open.

Not long after bringing the car home, Paul and I went to Roebling RaceTrack in Georgia where he drove on the track with a professional racecar driver beside him. The driver was surprised at how well Paul could handle the car and wanted to know how many times he had driven a Porsche. Paul replied, "Never, but I have driven it for over 20 years in my mind."

Twenty years of mental preparation. That's the kind of preparation that will help us, too, when problems come into our lives.

Do we spend as much time preparing ourselves for our Heavenly Home as we do on other things? Prepare your mind now and then when it comes time to stand up for Christ, it will be second nature.

Celebrate God for the gift of His Holy Word!

Study to shew thyself approved unto God, a workman that needeth not to be ashamed, rightly dividing the word of truth.

2 Timothy 2:15 (KJV)

Love Expressions

It was Sunday morning and the Emergency Department was overflowing with patients. We heard the telltale siren coming once again. The ambulance flew up the drive and almost before it stopped, a paramedic jumped out of the back with a small four-year-old boy. The boy, Alex, was in a continuous seizure. When his parents came in they told us Alex had a brain tumor and was only expected to live for a short time. He had been the recipient of a final wish from a charity: to visit his grandparents in Florida and go to Disney World. They had completed their Disney World adventure and had driven to our town to see his grandparents.

Alex was in very critical condition and we immediately called the pediatric hospital to come for him. In the meantime, we worked on stopping the seizures. All during the time we were caring for him, his mother stood beside him, crying and saying, "I should have done it before we left, I should have done it before we left." After hearing that several times, I asked her what it was that she should have done. She told me that before they left home she had gotten the supplies to make a model of Alex's hand for her to treasure after he was gone. She also kept asking Alex to wake up and tell her one more time that he loved her. She just wanted to hear it one more time, but he remained unconscious.

The team from the pediatric hospital was already on its way so there wasn't much time. I called home and asked my husband to hurry to a hobby store, get the model supplies, and come to our hospital as fast as possible. He did just that. After he arrived, he and Alex's father went to work to make the mold. They mixed up the modeling clay in a wash basin and put Alex's hand into it until it formed the mold that would later be filled with the Plaster of Paris.

They had barely finished with that procedure when the special team arrived. They loaded Alex on their stretcher and left for the pediatric hospital. We sent the wash basin along with his parents and hoped that it would be salvageable.

On the following Tuesday, we received a call from Alex's mother. She told us that Alex had been stabilized enough to fly home and had passed away that morning in his own bed. Then, she and her husband got around to pouring the Plaster of Paris into the mold. When it hardened, they cut the mold from around the hand model. To their surprise and joy, they said that Alex's hand model came out in the shape of "I love you" in sign language. No attempt had been made to do that, it just happened. Or was there a Divine presence there that acknowledged and answered a mother's prayer to have her son tell her one more time that he loved her?

Celebrate God for a wash basin of clay!

Truly, the God of Israel
loves His people and saves them.
He is the God who cannot be seen
because He hides Himself.

Isaiah 45:15 (The Clear Word)

Exactly Eleven

*H*ouses in Florida often have a lanai. This is a tropical name for a screened in back porch. The lanai is not included in the central air-conditioning for the house because it is open to the outside. The first house we bought in Florida had a lanai. After moving into the house we made a discovery: In the winter it was too cold to be on the lanai and in the summer it was too hot. Also, in the summer it was often wet and messy from the rain splashing mud in from the yard. It was not a very good area for our children to play in and also not very easy to keep clean. I would put on a bathing suit, get the hose and a brush, and scrub the floor and walls to try to get ahead of the mess. We were not the first ones to notice this situation. All around our neighborhood there were examples of houses where the lanai had been enclosed by windows. Usually these were jalousie windows that opened out in three or four sections. What a nice idea, we thought. It would make the room actually usable. However, having just purchased the house, we needed to save some money before tearing it up. We began saving for the windows. Paul is quite a handyman and planned to do the work himself so we only needed to save for the actual materials. He measured the area, drew his plans, and started figuring out how to do the project. It would require eleven of those jalousie windows. Adding up the supply cost, we decided that we would need around $2,000 to get started.

Time went by as we saved and finally we had the money we needed. We decided to go on vacation before starting the construction. Our travels took us to West Virginia where we attended a small church. During that service, the pastor made an appeal for funds for their church school. The school had been visited by state authorities and they had been told there were a lot of repairs that had to be made in the school building in order for them to pass inspection to open for the coming year.

After the service we talked about the school's needs and wanted to help. We didn't have a lot of money with us and, of course, no money budgeted for this project. But we could look back and see how God had blessed us in so many ways; we wanted to pass on the blessing. We thought about our savings for the windows and decided we would give that money for the school. After all, our lanai wasn't critical and we could begin saving again. We wrote a check and sent it to the school.

At the same time, the hospital where I worked was experiencing a parking problem. To expand the parking area, they had bought as many of the adjoining lots as possible and were tearing down the houses. A note was put in the hospital newsletter that any employee could go to these old houses and take anything they found they could use. When we got home from our vacation, only one of these old houses was still standing. One afternoon I went over to see it and guess what? It had jalousie windows that no one had spoken for. Eleven of them! Coincidence? I don't think so.

Celebrate God in ordinary windows!

To every thing there is a season,
and a time to every purpose
under the heaven:

Ecclesiastes 3:1 (KJV)

Trivia Expert

*H*ey Mom, did you know that…? This came from our son, Paul. We could have been riding in the car, sitting at the dinner table, or just about anywhere when he would ask this type of question. Often my answer was, "How do you know all of this stuff?" He would respond, "Don't you remember the third grade?" Oh yes, I do.

Soon after the school year began, Paul came home with a reading assignment from his teacher. I don't remember the exact assignment but it had to do with improving the student's reading skills. For some of the students this was quite a challenge, but for Paul it would be simple. He really enjoyed reading and would read anything that he could get his hands on. There were always stacks of library books in our home, and he loved to settle down in a chair and get "into" a good book. How could this assignment be turned into a learning experience for him?

On our porch was a bookcase that held a complete set of encyclopedias. Looking at them, inspiration came to me. I explained to Paul that the assignment for him would be to read at least an hour a day from the encyclopedias. After that, he could settle in with any of his other books. He wasn't thrilled with the idea, but began somewhat reluctantly with the letter A. As the year progressed, so did his journey through the alphabet. In fact, that year he completed reading the entire set.

Third grade was a long time ago, but he still surprises us with the bits of information that he gleaned from that year. He likes to kid me and say that I was unfair to him to expect all of that trivia reading; but he also has shared that having some of that knowledge has helped him with conversations at school and at work. Our son learned a lot from those reference books.

Just think of all that is in God's Reference Book! We have been told that if we read and learn scriptures now, when a time of crisis comes; we will be able to call to mind the verses and promises that we have read. God promises that our time in the Word will be a blessing to us when we need it the most.

Celebrate God for our ability to remember!

I remember your ancient precepts and find comfort in them for the present.
Psalm 119:52 (The Clear Word)

Aggravations

It had been a long day. Leaving early with a vanload of fifth and sixth grade students had been fun but now the activities were all over, the kids were tired and cranky, and the drive back had been long. Arriving at the school parking lot, I anxiously looked for the parents who were to be there to pick up their children. Notices had been sent out with the precise time and location so that the pick-up would go smoothly. The parents arrived. The students jumped into their cars and left. One by one the kids in my van were also picked up. That is, all of them but one. Soon there was no one left in the parking lot but my children and one girl. She was waiting for her father to come and he was nowhere in sight. Time dragged on. Fifteen minutes, half an hour, an hour, and still no father. The school was locked and there was no way to make a telephone call (these being the days before cell phones). We waited another thirty minutes and finally he came. His daughter jumped into his car and they were off.

Now we could begin our chores for the afternoon. At that time we had about two acres of ground to mow and each of our children had a section to do. It took a long time to cut the grass and we were already about two hours late getting started. Amy jumped on the riding mower and started out toward her section. Just as she was pulling out onto the driveway, a long snake slithered onto the same drive. Now, this was not an ordinary driveway. It was the access road to commercial buildings and was designed for tractor trailers. As the snake crawled onto the fourteen-foot-wide pavement, we noticed that it took up about one half of the drive. Seven feet! The snake had lovely large diamonds on it's skin and a rack of rattlers that measured over three inches in length.

As a nurse, I have seen patients that have been bitten by rattlesnakes. I have also read of people that were bitten by a snake because they had gotten too close while riding a lawnmower.

What if that father had arrived on time for his daughter? What if Amy had started out to do her mowing while the snake was just resting or curled up in the grass in her section? What if she hadn't seen the snake or been too close to it before noticing it? If the snake had not decided to sun itself on the drive at that time, we would not have seen it until perhaps it was too late.

As we were recovering from the scare, I began to put the afternoon in perspective. That aggravation didn't seem so bad now that I was able to see the whole picture. Perhaps it was even planned by Amy's guardian angel to protect her from injury. We don't always have the answers to why things don't go as planned, but we can surely strive to put all of our life into perspective.

Celebrate God for the little aggravations!

*The angel of the Lord encampeth
round about them that fear him,
and delivereth them.*

Psalm 34:7 (KJV)

Pauline

*B*efore our first child was born we moved to Punta Gorda, Florida. It happened that our house was across the street from the only other house in that area. That other house belonged to Pauline and Dick. They had retired early because of health reasons and moved to Florida to enjoy the sunshine and the absence of snow. As soon as we arrived, Pauline and Dick were over to see us and to welcome us to the area. At that time, they counted their family as four children, sixteen grandchildren, and three great-grandchildren. Large enough by anyone's standards, but not too large to include two more "children" who had just arrived in town. They gave us all sorts of suggestions about what to do, where to go, and how to settle into the area.

As we would visit, Pauline would tell us about all of her family in Iowa and show us the presents she had for them. She spent all year going to sales and looking for bargains. She always had a room full of gifts wrapped and labeled for the next occasion that was coming up. You can imagine what that room looked like before Christmas.

As Christmas was approaching, so was the birth of our daughter. To Dick's joy, Amy was born on December 27—which was his birthday as well. That made her very special to him and soon after her arrival, Pauline and Dick came over with a wind-up swing for her. She was added to their long and ever growing list of family. When our son, Paul, arrived 19 months later, he was also added to their list. Every year, no matter where we were or where they were, gifts would arrive on time for each of our children's birthdays and for Christmas. In addition to being on time, the gifts would often be articles of clothing and never once was a gift the wrong size. How did she do that? She was buying gifts and clothes for at least 25 people!

As long as we lived in the same town, I could count on a telephone call from Pauline as one of our birthday's was approaching. She would call to find a convenient time for us to come over for cake and ice cream to celebrate the occasion.

After several years, Dick passed away and we moved to a different town not too far away. Nothing changed. Pauline remembered every occasion. The gifts and cake and ice cream continued to be shared. In time, Pauline remarried and she was quick to tell her new husband, Bob, about her surrogate family in the next town. Gifts, cake, and ice cream kept coming.

Now her official numbers are up to four children, sixteen grandchildren, thirty-two great-grandchildren, and eight great-great-grandchildren! Pauline has been widowed again and is in her ninetieth year. She is still baking and giving gifts. She needs some help from her children now to keep everyone straight, but her family remains a top priority. And guess what? Her family has *six* children, not *four,* and *eighteen* grandchildren, not *sixteen,* because she still remembers us and considers us part of her family. She never forgot, not even once.

Celebrate God for faithful friends!

Good people do good things
because of the good in their hearts.
Luke 6:45 (CEV)

Foiled Robbery

On a business trip to Indiana my husband, Paul, was robbed. He had left the van for only a short time and returned to find the window broken and his briefcase and camera case stolen. The briefcase was bad enough because it had all of his business papers in it, but the real heart breaker was his camera case. In it, he had his special camera and some additional lenses. The camera was his pride and joy.

He called the local police and reported the robbery, giving them all of the serial numbers for the missing items. They didn't hold out much hope, but said they would investigate. He also called our insurance carrier to report the loss. The insurance agent asked about the price of the different items that would need replacing and was surprised at the amount. Paul explained to him that the camera came under the category of rare cameras and suggested that he call around to verify the cost.

Paul was still pretty sad when he returned home and told us about the loss. He recounted how the police said it was very unlikely that the items would ever be recovered. We waited to hear from the police, but after a week or so, there still was no news.

Our daughter, Amy, was very small and did not like seeing her Daddy unhappy. At our evening prayer time, she suggested that we ask Jesus to get the camera back. Paul and I looked at each other and agreed. We bowed our heads and she prayed, saying, "Dear Jesus, please get Daddy's camera back for him. Amen."

Now we had a dilemma. The police said it wouldn't be found and Amy was positive that her prayer would take care of everything. How would we be able to help her understand when no camera appeared?

Several more weeks went by, and one day Paul received a call from our insurance agent. He told Paul that the camera had been found and was being sent to Florida by the police in Indiana. Apparently the thief had taken the camera to a pawnshop and the pawnbroker had called the same rare camera dealer that our agent had called in order to find out what it was worth. The camera dealer was suspicious since there are not that many of this particular type of camera, so he compared the serial numbers and discovered that the camera was Paul's!

We were amazed, we couldn't believe that it was actually found and coming home. We also expressed this disbelief in Amy's presence. This surprised her because she had never even considered that it wouldn't be returned. After all, she had asked Jesus for help. Her only comment was: "I should have asked for your brief-case, too!" How small was our faith and how great was hers.

Celebrate God for a child's faith!

To have faith means to be confident of the things we hope for and to be sure of the things we can't see.

Hebrews 11:1 (The Clear Word)

Account Ability

For as long as I can remember I have been active in my church. This has included teaching an adult class, being a superintendent in the adult area, being a deaconess or a greeter, and so on. You get the picture. These duties were related to the service and were performed during that time.

When Amy, and later, Paul, were born it was difficult, if not impossible, to be available to do these duties. For a while I helped in the Cradle Roll department but soon discovered that was not my gift. I was accustomed to dealing with adults. Singing songs with little hand puppets just did not seem to suit my style nor did the children respond to my efforts.

Still wanting to be of service to the church, I asked the pastor if there was a task that I could perform at home. This would allow me to be with my children during the church service. He asked if I would be willing to be the assistant treasurer. I am a registered nurse, not an accountant. I took one semester of bookkeeping in high school and had no accounting experience and very little mathematics education. The pastor explained that this position would mainly be to count the offerings received at the church service and to write an occasional check if the treasurer should be away. That didn't sound too difficult and after praying about it, I accepted the job of assistant treasurer.

Our church was fairly large and the amount of money to count each week was always several thousand dollars. The children's departments were great for turning in large jars of pennies or cards with nickels or dimes stuck to them. All of this had to be sorted, counted, rolled, and tallied up for the treasurer to enter into the church's books. The first time I saw the books, I thought of how thankful I was that my job was only counting the money! After all, double entry accounting was not a term I even knew existed.

You guessed it! Less than a month after agreeing to be the assistant, the treasurer announced that he and his wife were moving to another state. He had been the treasurer for years and hadn't given any indication that his situation would be changing. When he arrived at our house to turn over the books, I almost panicked. There were large, double entry ledgers, checking accounts and savings accounts I had to learn about. He also brought a huge old-fashioned adding machine, the kind that you pulled a handle for each entry and it printed out the numbers on a roll of paper. To me it looked like an antique, but he loved it dearly and said it was much more accurate than any calculator. It was also guaranteed to wake up any napping children and make them want to help pull the handle. What had I gotten myself into? I wanted to go directly to the pastor and resign, but with our family "no-quitting" policy that was not an option. Resigning would not be a good example for our children.

So, I waded in where angels would fear to tread. Each week I spent all of my waking moments that the children were *not* awake dealing with all that this new responsibility involved. Counting and sorting the money was time consuming but not too difficult. The books were another story. For me, it was torture to keep adding and checking until all of the columns balanced up and down as well as across. Since I had no formal training in accounting, and no one to assist me in this work, I wasted long hours doing things over and over again. Because it was church money, and therefore confidential, I couldn't even turn to my husband for assistance.

Somehow I survived that year. The church auditor came at the end of the year to audit the books. He was impressed with the accuracy of the columns, but I think he got an ulcer from my answers to his questions about how I arrived at the figures that were there. By mutual consent, we decided that someone else should take over the responsibility.

About that time, my husband started his own business. This had always been his dream. We decided that since the children were still young and not requiring as much money as they later would, this was the time to venture out. My part in the process, believe it or not, consisted of being the secretary/treasurer for our newly formed corporation. Once again, I was faced with the double entry situation, but this time I knew what to do. When we sold the business, the accountants all had good things to say about how the money had been handled and recorded.

I am in awe that the year I spent agonizing over the church books was the year that prepared me for my future responsibility to our business. My prayers about accepting that assistant treasurer role were answered in ways that I had not imagined. The church year ended just in time for our business year to begin. Even the timing was perfect. A small thing but truly awesome!

Celebrate God for His timing!

Whatsoever thy hand findeth to do,
do it with thy might.

Ecclesiastes 9:10 (KJV)

Afternoon Squall

It was a gorgeous afternoon on Charlotte Harbor. The sky was bright blue with fluffy white clouds everywhere and the breeze was blowing just right. As the new owners of a sailboat, we were anxious to get out on the water. We had taken the Coast Guard sailing course and learned a great deal, but there is no substitute for actually being out on the water. Today looked like the perfect day to begin our sailing adventures.

The four of us put on our life jackets. Then it was time to cast off. The wind was wonderful. It caught in the sails and we were making great time as we sped out across the harbor. With the sun shining and the wind whipping by, we felt like we were in Heaven.

After an hour or so, we decided it was time to turn around and head back to shore. As we came about, we had our first glimpse of the sky that had been behind us. There was a reason for the lovely wind that we had experienced. In the distance, not too far back, there was a big dark cloud blowing toward us. As we watched, the wind increased and soon we were having difficulty keeping the boat going in the correct direction. We also began to see some lightning, hear thunder, and knew that one of Florida's famous afternoon thunderstorms was almost upon us. What could we do? This had not been covered in our classes and we were novices on the water!

Our children were our main concern. They were frightened by the loud noise, the rain, and the choppy water; so were we. Going below into the cabin, they both started to cry. I couldn't leave them down there alone, so I went below to be with them. That left my husband in the cockpit by himself fighting with the wheel and trying to control the boat. Down in the cabin we talked about the storm and the fact that their dad knew a lot about the boat, how to sail, and that he would get us safely to shore. We said a few short prayers and waited. The storm continued and after some time, I realized that I had not heard our son, Paul, say anything for a while. Looking back at the V-berth, I saw him sound asleep. The storm was violent and we were pitching around in the water but he felt safe enough to go to sleep. His dad was out in the storm taking care of everything and he didn't need to worry because Dad was there. He trusted his earthly father. How much more we can trust our Heavenly Father to lead us through life's storms!

Celebrate God for those we can trust!

In the Lord put I my trust.

Psalms 11:1 (KJV)

Eye of the Beholder

*T*hey say that beauty is in the eye of the beholder. That seems to be true. What is beautiful to one person may not be to another. Bonnie arrived in the United States from the Philippines. She was moving here to work as a nurse in the Chicago area. The climate in Chicago is quite different from her homeland and so the flowers and shrubs were new to her. She had a new home and was very interested in making it pretty by planting flowers in the yard. Because of her low budget, she looked around for plants she could move from the wild to her garden. After a few weeks, she invited several of us to come over to see her new place. She was especially proud of the lovely flower garden she had planted. There in the front yard were the flowers she had found and transplanted. Prominent among the floral presentations were multiple bright shiny yellow flowers, her favorites. She reported to us that even though they were very difficult to dig up and move she had liked them so much that it was worth all of the work.

Just then, one of our group started to smile. She

told Bonnie that the yellow flowers were just weeds and problem weeds at that. They were dandelions! And Bonnie had planted them all over the place. She told Bonnie that she was going to have a lot of problems getting rid of them. I was rather proud of Bonnie. Instead of being hurt or embarrassed she just repeated that she thought they were lovely. She said that since God created them, they were perfect and she was happy to have them. In her eye, she beheld beauty. The next time you see a dandelion, take a minute to really appreciate it and you may also see the beauty that Bonnie saw.

One time our family was at a state park and our daughter and I took about a two-mile walk. Starting out, we walked and talked together and didn't pay much attention to our surroundings other than to notice the general beauty. After a while we noticed a pretty wild-flower and stopped to examine it. Then, we saw several more. We decided to count the different kinds of wild-flowers that we saw on this short walk. We found 38 different types! They were yellow, white, red, purple, blue, and several varying shades of each of those colors. What a gorgeous garden, full of different colors and a variety of shapes.

As we were walking, several cars passed us. At the speed they were driving it probably was impossible for them to see the lovely floral display. In fact, one car stopped and asked us what we were looking at. Had we seen a deer or some other animal? We pointed out some of the flowers we were enjoying and the driver said to his passengers, "Oh, just some wildflowers, nothing important."

They missed out. God has prepared a blessing for all who take the time to notice the everyday things He has given us.

Celebrate God for weeds and wildflowers!

He hath made every thing beautiful in his time:

Ecclesiastes 3:11 (KJV)

Six Trombones

*P*ort Charlotte, Florida, has a community band. Since the area is primarily populated with retirees, the band is made up predominately of senior citizens, many of whom were music teachers or band directors. They get together every Tuesday evening to practice and perform monthly concerts in a local auditorium. The price for the concerts is $2.00 per person and they are performed in the early afternoon so that the participants, as well as the audience, can afford to attend and drive home before dark. Occasionally, there is a high school student that joins the band, but the program is really geared to the senior citizens.

When our son, Paul, was in the eighth grade, he played the trombone. He didn't like to sing and had difficulty carrying a tune. Since music is such an important part of life and since singing was probably not going to work for him, we suggested he try an instrument. He chose the trombone. It seemed a difficult choice. I had thought more of an instrument where finger position determined the note, not one that needed the player to be able to hear the sound and move the slide to just the correct position. But he loved that trombone. He would practice even without reminders and would often call out to me, "Mom, do you recognize that song?" Since the trombone practically never has the melody, it was almost impossible to know what the song was and if he was getting the sound correct.

At the beginning of Paul's eighth grade year, he heard about the community band. He asked his school's band director about playing in it and she arranged for him to try out. They had never had a member so young, only 12, and weren't real sure that it would work. To their credit, they gave him a chance. He loved that band. Tuesday night wasn't the best night for a schoolboy to be at a band practice but, that didn't matter to him. If he had a test on Wednesday or a lot of homework to do, he made sure he got it all done in time for practice. Once, he was not feeling very well and I suggested that he skip that night's practice. He would have none of that, saying he felt just fine. He never missed a practice or a concert that entire year.

The trombone section consisted of six members, Paul and five retired men, some of whom had been band directors. They really took him under their wing. He became their project and they taught him all they could about the trombone.

One Sunday afternoon the concert had a selection that featured the trombone section in a group solo. When the time came, all six of the trombonists got up from their section and came out to the front to play their solo. There were some ladies sitting behind me. I could hear them talking about the young boy up there playing along with the older, gray-haired gentlemen. They became more and more excited and at one point, one of them nudged me on the shoulder and said, "Can you see that young man up there?" He was quite a hit.

At the last concert of the year, Paul was given a solo to play all by himself with only some background from the band. He walked to the front of the auditorium, stood very assuredly and professionally, and looked at the band director. The director raised the baton and signaled for the music to begin. Paul played the piece perfectly and was greeted with a standing ovation when he finished. Those wonderful retired men were grinning from ear to ear and looking quite pleased with themselves. As well they should be. They had been willing to take a chance, as well as the time and energy, to help a young man grow and develop. And he blossomed under their care.

Celebrate God for our mentors!

And whatsoever ye do, do it heartily,
as to the Lord, and not unto men;

Colossians 3:23 (KJV)

Perseverance Pays

In the third grade, our daughter, Amy, decided that she would like to play the flute. At school the band didn't begin until fourth grade, so she was out of luck there. However, my philosophy has always been to practice the theory of "carpe diem" so, after some searching, we found a high school music teacher who gave private lessons. A trip to the music store got us a rented flute and off we went to the first lesson. After the time allotted, Amy was unable to make a sound on the flute. The teacher suggested that she spend the next week of practice trying to get a sound to come out of the instrument. Every day after school, Amy would come home and blow and blow without any results. For two weeks, this continued until she was very frustrated and thought about quitting. At our house, we do not believe in quitting. We told Amy that if she took lessons and practiced for three months and then still wanted to stop the lessons, we would not consider that quitting. She kept up the blowing and one day a sound came out of the flute! It wasn't much of a sound, just a squeal, but still a sound. We were all very excited about that little sound.

She continued her lessons and we got used to the squeal of the flute. Fourth grade came and she was able to join the school band. Band became a large part of her life from then through high school, and was the means of her winning several awards as well as taking trips to Sweden and Germany. She finished out high school as first chair piccolo in addition to playing the flute. Her life was enriched because she persisted, even when there was no sound to be heard from her flute. She did not quit! She kept trying and trying until she won!

Celebrate God for perseverance!

I press toward the mark
for the prize of the high calling
of God in Christ Jesus.
Philippians 3:14 (KJV)

Musical Shoes

*D*uring the eighth grade, our daughter, Amy, went to a school that had very professional-looking band uniforms. They were blue and white with gold trim. The band members all glowed as they marched around in uniform. In addition to the outfit, the uniform consisted of white shoes for both the boys and the girls. My, did they look good when they were dressed up!

That year, one of Amy's best friends was Judy. She played the oboe and sat near Amy in the front row of the band. On the day of a big band concert, Amy came home from school and asked if I thought it would be all right for her to wear black shoes at the concert. The question made no sense to me as we had just bought her a new pair of white shoes that she really liked. She had been so excited when trying them on with her uniform. I asked Amy why she wanted to wear black shoes and after some prodding, she told me that Judy's mother was having some real difficulties making ends meet and that she could not afford to buy new white shoes. She said that she thought Judy would feel better if she didn't have to be the only one sitting on the front row not wearing white shoes.

I was very touched by Amy's caring and thoughtfulness, but hoped to find a better solution. That afternoon, Amy and I went shopping again. We bought a pair of shoes for Judy that was exactly like Amy's pair. Time had run out and it was time for the performance. When we arrived at the concert hall, Judy was there in her blue and white with gold trim uniform trying not to let her black shoes show any more than necessary. Amy gave the white shoes to her and they both cried and hugged while Judy changed from her black shoes to the white ones. To this day, I am not sure how well those shoes actually fit her. However, I will always remember the smiles on the girls' faces as they sat on the front row that night playing their instruments with gusto and pushing their feet out for all to see.

Celebrate God for an ordinary pair of shoes!

Even a child is known by his doings,
whether his work be pure,
and whether it be right.
Proverbs 20:11 (KJV)

73

Advanced Cycling

*B*oth of our children began riding bicycles when they were four years old. Their father was quite an enthusiast and wanted them to enjoy the pleasure of riding like he did. When Amy was four years old we bought her a bicycle and her dad began the lessons. He wanted her to learn without using training wheels which would give her better balance, he thought. It worked! They would go up and down the street and, after a few troubling sessions, Amy caught on to the procedure. Then a couple of years later, Paul got his bicycle and had the same lessons. From that point on, we became a biking family.

While the kids were in elementary school, their father proposed an adventure in cycling. They began working on a plan to ride their bicycles from the southernmost point of land in Florida up to the northernmost point of land right across the river from the Georgia border. The total mileage of this adventure clocked in at 606 miles. An ambitious task! They planned to ride along A1A, the coastal road, as much as possible.

Preparation for the trip began when both of the

children learned how to completely disassemble and then reassemble their entire bikes. Of course they learned all about fixing flat tires, too. Each of the bicycles had a small pouch on the back which was loaded with one change of clothes for each of them. Items such as toothpaste, brushes, shampoo, etc., were divided among the pouches, leaving no room for anything else. The plan was for them to ride as far as they could each day and then stop at a motel for the night. No one would be following along in a car, so they were really on their own with only their bicycles and each other.

When all preparations were complete, we drove to Key West where they dipped their front wheels in the water by the marker announcing the southernmost point of Florida. Then, off they went. I drove home and waited for a call from them to tell me they were ready to be picked up. It took ten days, one of which they didn't do any riding and one marathon day of over 100 miles.

On the 100-mile day, they were riding along Hutchinson Island and there were no motels to be found. They were also trying to out-ride a thunderstorm that had caught up to them around mile 80 with no stopping place in sight. Their dad suggested that they pray and ask that the storm not arrive until they could get to some sort of shelter. According to Amy, as soon as they got to a shelter, the rain began in torrents.

Another title for this story could have been "Memories," because that was their dad's motivation for the ride. We both thought that it was very important to make family memories and looked for ways to do that. And it worked!

Today, fifteen years later, if we are driving along A1A with either Paul or Amy, they will all of a sudden say, "See that place over there? That is where we got a sandwich." Or maybe, "See that shelter? That is where we took a rest break." When we pass a motel they stayed in, they like to remind their dad that at the end of a long day, he would crash on the bed and they would put on their swimsuits and go to the pool. They have many positive memories of that trip. They enjoyed it enough that the next summer they rode across Florida from the edge of the panhandle, Pensacola, to the Eastern Shore, St. Augustine. They remember each trip and recall vividly things that happened along the way.

We are on a journey, also. Our walk with Jesus is an adventure and He has given us His book to help us learn about Him. We need active time with His Word and with our Heavenly Dad in prayer to connect with those wonderful promises.

Celebrate God for memories!

Some trust in chariots, and some in horses: but we will remember the name of the Lord our God.

Psalms 20:7 (KJV)

Taking Flight

One summer when our children were in grade school, we brought home all sorts of boxes of different sizes and shapes. So many boxes, in fact, that they were all over the backyard. The largest was a refrigerator box. During that summer our children, along with all of the neighborhood children, had a great time building a city out of cardboard. The girls spent time inside of the boxes coloring window curtains and doing paintings for the walls. The boys were more interested in the outside. They connected the boxes, built a steeple for the church, doors and counter tops for the stores, and so on. Our son, Paul, rigged the "town" with all sorts of strings and pulleys. For example, he could pull a string that would open a door that in turn would let a shelf down that would then raise a flag for the mailbox. He even had an airplane that landed on one of the boxes. That entire summer the kids cut, pasted, colored, and arranged those boxes to their heart's content. The only down side was getting all of the boxes safely into the porch and garage before the afternoon rains would come and then hauling them all out again when the ground dried.

During that summer, we noticed that Paul was very good at figuring out different approaches and inventing different ways to make things work. This was all verified when he came home from school one day. He had a note saying that he needed to write the sentence, "I will make more constructive use of my time" a thousand times.

He told me that the reason for this disciplinary action was that he had rigged up a security system around his desk using rubber bands and spitballs. If anyone tried to get into his desk or move his belongings, a rubber band would be triggered to fire a spitball through the air at the intruder. Actually, I thought that was a pretty constructive use of time, especially since he was not behind on any of his work and was getting excellent grades. At least he was using his time without bothering any of his fellow students. Anyway, the sentences turned out not to be too big of a deal because he wrote them using three pencils at a time and thus cut the chore in thirds.

He "built" multiple airplanes out of paper, sticks, and even blades of grass as a small boy. He then graduated to making models of airplanes and setting off model rockets that he had built. As he got older, his method of making airplanes may have changed, but his enthusiasm never did. In high school, he became interested in remote control planes and by college he was building his own model planes to fly.

As children grow, friends and acquaintances always ask them: "What are you going to do when you grow up?"

or "What are you going to take in college?" For the most part, kids have no idea. I know that Paul went from wanting to be a fireman to an English teacher, from being a business entrepreneur to working for an outfitter tying flies for fishing.

Even though I had ample evidence through Paul's younger years, it still came as a bit of a surprise to me when he decided to go to graduate school and major in aeronautics and astronautics. The ever-present evidence of airplanes of different sorts and in different stages of development should have been a real clue, but I missed it. I had overlooked the talents and abilities that he had in this area. Are you overlooking anything?

Celebrate God for our talents!

Trust in the Lord with all thine heart;
and lean not unto thine own understanding.
In all thy ways aknowledge him,
and he shall direct thy paths.

Proverbs 3:5-6 (KJV)

Fashion Statement

ighth grade graduation was approaching. The students were excited and the girls were discussing what they would be wearing for the BIG day. They had put in eight long years of study and were ready to celebrate. For the actual graduation service, caps and gowns would be worn, but the girls all knew that the reception after the ceremony was the really important time. They had to be decked out in all their glory for the benefit of the guys, plus teachers, parents, and friends. For months conversation would automatically turn to, "What are you going to wear?"

My college roommate taught me how to knit and ever since then, I have made afghans, sweaters, slippers and so on. Since my roommate was a perfectionist, she had me redo every stitch until it was almost impossible to tell if it was done by hand or bought in a store. My stitches and tension were nearly perfect before she would declare that the item was properly made.

I had knitted several items for Amy through the years and as graduation got closer she asked me if I would knit her a dress for the big day. I felt that was quite a compliment and started looking for patterns and yarn. We examined lots of options before she finally decided what she wanted. She chose a lovely pattern, a sheath dress that got its shape from increasing or decreasing stitches at the appropriate places. The pattern began at the hem and worked its way up on a circular needle to a rolled collar all done in a cable stitch. After she chose the pattern we started to look for yarn. That in itself was no easy task as it required many, many skeins of yarn. Finally, Amy chose a beautiful magenta color, which we ordered.

The yarn arrived and then the work began. For six weeks I was covered in magenta yarn. I took the dress with me to soccer games, school committee meetings, pretty much everywhere. There was a deadline that had to be met and the work began to show results. It was exciting to watch the dress grow from the hem up to, and including, the collar. What was more exciting was to see Amy try it on for the first time and realize that it was a perfect fit. With her blue eyes and long blond hair, she was quite a knockout in it. We were able to find a pair of shoes that matched her dress exactly. She was now ready for the big day to arrive and I was ready to retire from knitting for a while. Even though 5'6" may not seem all that tall, it is a lot of distance to cover one stitch at a time.

A week or so before graduation, Amy decided to wear her special dress to church. She was excited about her new outfit and wanted her friends to see it. At church, we were all standing in the lobby when a girl about Amy's age came over to see her. Amy was quick to tell her that she was wearing her graduation dress and that her mother had made it. Instead of being happy for Amy, the girl's comment was, "I wouldn't wear that dress, it's homemade. Couldn't your folks afford to buy you a nice new dress?" Amy's facial expression sort of changed and even though she was still smiling and pointing out to this girl that she would rather have this dress than any other one, it was easy to tell that she was hurt by the comment.

This particular girl had graduated the year before and worn a designer dress that had cost her folks a small fortune. To her, labels were everything and homemade was to be avoided at all costs.

Amy wore that magenta dress for her graduation and received many, many compliments on how beautiful she looked. However, the harm had been done. What could have been a memorable occasion with a very special outfit was somewhat tainted by careless, mean words. Words can be overcome and we do move on, but at what cost? Amy kept that dress for years, mainly, I think, because she loves me and appreciated the work that went into it; however, it could never be a real favorite of hers again.

For some of us it is easy to remember the unkind things that happen. Something small in the course of a lifetime but remembered for many years can affect our outlook on life. One definition of forgiveness is to let go.

We may think we have forgiven but until we ask God for the ability to let go, we still have work to do. It may be impossible for us to forget, but if we let go of the hurt, forgiveness is ours.

Celebrate God as He helps us learn to let go!

Be not rash with thy mouth,
and let not thine heart be hasty
to utter any thing before God:
for God is in heaven,
and thou upon earth:
therefore let thy words be few.

Ecclesiastes 5:2 (KJV)

Daily Devotion

*W*hen our children were small, we made a concerted effort to provide them with Bible stories. We bought several sets of books and cassette tapes that contained the stories of Bible characters and also stories of contemporary people that were positive and uplifting. We read the same stories over and over again. There were several of these that became favorites and I imagine that even today, Amy and Paul could probably follow along the tape about Daniel without missing very many of the words. So could their mother and father!

While our children were at home, it was relatively easy to influence what they read and listened to. Then along came school and the broadening of their horizons. Since they went to a Christian school, there was still a certain amount of supervision with their selection of reading materials. At home the old favorites were still around and continued to get more and more dog-eared as the years passed.

Our children moved from having everything read to them to reading for themselves. Each week, we would go to the library and get about twenty books for each of them to read. Many weeks we needed to make a second trip to the library. As you can imagine, both of our children became avid and excellent readers. Also, as they became older, we had less and less influence in their reading selections. We prayed and hoped that the guidance of their earlier years would continue to keep them interested in their daily devotions and spiritual reading.

For high school, our son packed his belongings and joined his sister at a Christian boarding school in Virginia. One concern I had when Paul left home was that boys could be very hard on a new student and would possibly make fun of him. At that time, Paul was continuing to have his own morning devotions and was reading his Bible. I wondered what response he would get from his roommate and the other fellows on his hall when they observed him reading and praying. I have known of other boys that gave up their devotions to try to fit in, to be liked, or just because it was too difficult to always try to explain what they were doing. These other boys often gave up more than just their devotions, they gave up their relationship with Jesus. My prayer was that Paul would continue and even grow in his relationship with his Creator.

One weekend when he came home, I asked Paul if he was having any problems at school or in the dormitory and he said "No." I then asked him if any of the boys had noticed him having his devotions and said anything. His answer was yes. "A few of the boys kind of laugh and make comments, but that is their problem, not mine," Paul said. I praise God for that answer!

Paul continued on in school. He went to a Christian college and after graduating he applied to graduate school. At the completion of his master's degree, the whole family assembled for his graduation. He was living in university housing and sharing an apartment with a fellow he had met there. When we walked into his apartment for the first time, it was immediately apparent where Paul sat at the table. There on his side of the table was his Bible. It was not hidden in his room or covered with something, it was in full view of anyone who would come to his place.

Paul is not a preacher or theologian, he is an engineer. His study of the Bible has no direct relationship to his livelihood. But it does have a direct relationship to his connection with Jesus and his ability to handle whatever comes his way. He very calmly goes through life without worrying about things that he can't change. As the world becomes more and more uncertain, what better way is there to remain calm and assured of God's presence in our world than to stay tuned to His Holy Word?

Celebrate God for our ability to connect with Him!

Keep your Creator in mind while you are young! In years to come, you will be burdened down with troubles and say, "I don't enjoy life anymore."
Ecclesiastes 12:1 (CEV)

Random Meeting

*P*aul and I wanted something nice that we could use to camp on weekends in the state parks near our home. We had looked at all sorts of motor homes and trailers, but couldn't find just the right thing. We wanted something small but yet comfortable and we had a list of hoped-for amenities. One day we drove by a dealership and saw a van that looked like a possibility. It was large enough to stand up in when the top was raised and we could park it in the garage when the top was down. The van had everything that was on our list! We were "struck" with it and went in to discuss a price with the salesman. We were able to put the deal together right then and drove the van home.

The very next weekend we were off to try it out at a park. We used the van often and really enjoyed it. We only saw one other van like it on the road and thought that perhaps the reason was that the van was such a specialty vehicle. We knew that it would be a difficult vehicle to sell, but that didn't bother us because it was perfect for us and we thought we would keep it forever.

In a year things changed. Paul was looking at a

new job opportunity that was perfect for him but would require us to move. We prayed about what we should do and he felt that he should take the job. The only problem was that this new job would require us to sell the van. Not only were we looking at taking quite a loss, but anyone we talked with said it was too expensive for them. We didn't have any answers so we decided to leave it all in God's hands and began preparing for the move.

In our town there is an ice cream store that I passed almost every day. To get your frozen treat, you walk up to a window and then eat it while sitting in your car. It had been almost 15 years since anyone in our family had stopped there but this particular day I felt like getting an ice cream treat. I went to the window, bought my ice cream, and headed back to the van. Just as I was getting in, a man walked up to me and asked if the van was mine. I replied that it was and he asked if he could look at it. He called his wife over and the two of them took a tour of the inside and outside of the van. Then without any warning, he said to me, "Is there any chance you might be willing to sell it?" I was shocked because there was no "for sale" sign on it. I said that it was for sale and he asked the price. Fortunately, Paul and I had talked about that previously, so I quoted the price to him. Without any discussion, he said, "We'll take it."

Why did I stop for ice cream just then? Why did these two people happen to be there and also in the market for just this type of vehicle? Some would say it was a coincidence, just a random meeting, but I would have to disagree. When we ask God to take charge of our lives and our decisions, why should we be surprised when He does just that? We shouldn't be. He does just what He has promised us that He will do!

Celebrate God for random meetings!

> *Getting to know God should be*
> *your first priority. He'll provide*
> *all your other necessities.*
> Luke 12:31 (The Clear Word)

Community Thanksgiving

*T*he whole point of Thanksgiving is to share gratitude. It is a time to think back and remember the multitude of blessings that we have received. It is also a time to share these memories with others.

Each Thanksgiving Day, my parents used to go around the dinner table and ask each of us to say something that we were particularly thankful for that year. Every year at the beginning of this ritual, my mother would tell of the year when I was very little and was asked that question. My answer was "my bed." Everyone seemed to think that was amusing and for years I had to hear the story over and over again. Each year the question brought forth more and more evidence of all the blessings that God had given us. We have much for which to be thankful.

As time passed, our family grew and we tried to be aware of things that we could do to help those around us. In the next town, there was a mission where I volunteered for several years. My job was to prepare dinner for those living at the mission and for the people who lived in a nearby low-income housing area. During this time, my daughter, Amy, and I got to know many of these people personally.

Thanksgiving was coming up and we decided to have a special dinner for them. There were about 50 people that would attend and we started cooking and preparing food. The only problem was the turkey. We are vegetarian and having never cooked any meat, let alone big turkeys; it was just too much. We checked with the food service director at the hospital where I worked and requested help. We asked if he could get permission to cook the turkeys for us if we bought them. Of course, he wanted to know all about what we were trying to do. He went to see the administrator and got permission not only to cook the turkeys, but to also contact one of their vendors to see if he could get them to donate the birds. The vendor was happy to help. The food service director cooked the turkeys, and also made all of the gravy. Then a friend found out about the dinner and volunteered to make pies.

What started out as a major project for Amy and me became so much easier because of all the people who jumped in to help out. The old adage, "Many hands make light work" is so true! We learned that if you want to see the good in people, just present them with the information they need and they will respond. We certainly saw evidence of that. Since we are vegetarians, it probably would have been better if we had also recruited some expertise for the carving of the turkeys! Amy and I each attacked one and learned that there must be a trick to the carving that we didn't know. I'm sure you can imagine what those slices looked like but no one seemed to mind!

Celebrate God for helping hands!

And he said,
The things which are impossible
with men are possible with God.
Luke 18:27 (KJV)

John Doe

*W*ith lights flashing, the ambulance arrived at the Emergency Department. The paramedics quickly unloaded a stretcher with a young man strapped onto it. He was unconscious but otherwise had no visual injuries. The history given to the staff was that this young man had been found in a ditch where his vehicle, a very fancy sports car, had rolled over and been destroyed. He had been wearing his seat belt which prevented him from being thrown from the car; however, he had hit his head hard enough to be knocked out. Apparently his wallet had not been in his pocket because no identification could be found. The accident had happened in a remote area and the ditch was full of water. After the ambulance had left with the young man, the Highway Patrol officers searched the area and found his belongings but no wallet. He was registered as John Doe and the treatment began.

To check him for injuries, his clothes were removed and one of the nurses made a comment about how expensive his apparel appeared to be, all designer items. His watch was an expensive brand

and his cell phone was the latest technology. When he was ready, he was sent for an X-ray and CT scan, and it was determined that his only injury was to his head. He was put in a quiet room and the observation began. That was when the speculation also began. Someone suggested that he must be a drug dealer because of his young age, the expensive sports car, and the cost of his personal items. All of the conversation was speculation as the law enforcement officers had not been able to make any identification.

After several hours, the young man woke up. He was somewhat dazed and confused about his surroundings, but seemed medically stable. We learned his name and that he had been on his way to Orlando (about 150 miles away) when the accident occurred. In time, the doctor determined that he was ready to be discharged from the Emergency Department and wrote the order. Now the young man had a problem. He had only the clothes he had come in with and they were wet and dirty. He was unable to make contact with anyone who he knew in Orlando and had no wallet, thus no money. As he was making calls on his expensive cell phone, the speculation began again and the consensus was that he must be a drug dealer. He didn't seem to have any family or friends that he could call to help him with his problem.

It was getting late and he needed to leave the Emergency Department. Then there was the problem of getting to Orlando. A call to the bus station gave us the rates and times of buses and the next one wasn't until the next day. A motel in town offered a low rate to hospital patients, so we called to reserve him a room. He was hungry, having not eaten for many hours, but we really didn't have much to offer.

After determining that food, lodging, and transportation were his basic needs, we determined that he could get to Orlando if he had $100. But he had nothing! I called home and asked my husband how much cash he could gather and could he possibly bring the money to the Emergency Department. During the call, the young man kept saying that he would pay me back when he got to Orlando. I overheard one nurse say, "Yeah, sure." Another nurse told me that I was an idiot and would never see the money again.

In a short time, our son, Paul, arrived at the Emergency Department. He was home from college for a visit and offered to bring the money. He didn't look much younger than our patient and I'm sure he could think of a thousand ways that he could use the money at school.

When he came in, he handed the money to our patient who again promised that he would repay it. Our son looked straight at him and said, "No, you don't need to repay this. Just promise me that someday when you see someone who is in need, you will pass it on." The patient took the money, got in a taxi, and left for the motel.

It has been several years since this happened and, no, we never heard from this young man again. We didn't expect to. We also never learned any more about him. Maybe he was a drug dealer, maybe not, but that is not important. What is important is that hopefully this kindness made a difference in his life. What if this small act is the only glimpse he has had of God's care? What if it changed his life even in a small way? What if?

Celebrate God for opportunities to show kindness!

Let brotherly love continue.
Be not forgetful to entertain strangers:
for thereby some have entertained
angels unawares.
Hebrews 13:1-2 (KJV)

Charlie

*T*here was no way to tell how old Charlie was. You could see him riding on his three-wheel bicycle around town and guess at his age, but it would only be a guess. He had obviously been injured at some time and walked with a very distinct limp. He also had long, straggly gray hair, a long, shaggy gray beard, and tattered clothing. The first time I met him was at a homeless shelter. He was soon asked to leave the shelter because of his drinking problem. There was a rule against having alcohol at the shelter, and he could not give up his bottle of hard liquor. It was always with him, wrapped in a brown paper bag in the basket of his bicycle along with an old ragged sweater and nothing else. After leaving the shelter, he lived on the streets. The police all knew him and turned the other way when they saw him lying on the ground by some tree at night. They didn't want to take him to jail and would sometimes even give him food.

When it rained, one of his favorite shelters was a picnic area at one of the parks in town. This park also had a great path right by the harbor and was one of our favorite places for walking. One day it started to rain while we were walking and we found ourselves taking shelter in the same picnic area as Charlie. Usually he would ride quickly away if anyone came near him, but this day the rain kept all of us pinned in under the cover. As we sat there we began to talk. Charlie opened up and told the story of his life. He had been a jet engine mechanic during World War II and had a wife and three children. He must have been pretty intelligent because jets were new then and to be trained on them would have required some effort on his part. He said that he had been planning to make the military his career and had re-enlisted several times. I don't remember the rank he said he obtained before he began drinking.

He then went on to say that drinking had caused him to lose everything. His wife left him and took the children. The military tried to help him with his alcohol problem and when they couldn't, they discharged him. He had been in the military long enough to get a pension and that was how he supported his drinking habit. He would rather have the liquor than a place to live.

That particular rainy evening he had on his ragged sweater and was still shivering. He wouldn't tell us where he planned to sleep in the rain but it was obvious that he had no covers. We told him to stay at the shelter and we would go home and get a blanket for him. We didn't know if he really would stay there because his habit was to disappear instead of being with other people. We took the chance, though, and went home, took the blanket off of our son's bed, and drove back to the park armed with the blanket and a sandwich for him. He was still there! We gave him our small gift and left.

For many months after that evening, I would see Charlie riding around town with the bottle in the brown paper bag and the blanket in his basket. Once I saw him lying under a tree wrapped in that blanket. We never had any more conversations, I think he was embarrassed that he had shared so much of himself with us.

Then, one day a police officer told me that Charlie had been found dead the previous night lying under a tree wrapped in a worn and dirty blanket. It was just an old torn, dirty piece of fabric but it was a comfort to him. That blanket meant nothing to us, but I pray that it was a means to show Charlie, in some small way, a glimpse of a loving God.

Celebrate God with an ordinary blanket!

Come unto me, all ye that labour and are heavy laden, and I will give you rest.
Matthew 11:28 (KJV)

Spirit of Giving

Christmas was just around the corner. There was the usual hustle and bustle with shopping and searching for just the right gifts. Sometimes it is hard to remember the real reason for Christmas when we are caught up in all of the activity.

At home the Christmas tree went up and our small children watched in awe as it became transformed from a tree to a thing of beauty with all of the decorations. The skirt was in place at the base of the tree, and the little ceramic village was laid out on it. Then came the question that all children ask: "Where are the presents?" Christmas is about the greatest present we could ever have, the gift of a Savior. But this is a hard concept to get across to small children who watch all of the feverish activity that does not seem to coincide with that great gift. It's easy for them to see Christmas as all about them and what they will be getting. To teach them about Jesus' birth, salvation, and how to love and give at this time of year is a real challenge.

That year, when the question about the presents was asked, we were ready with a suggestion. Our children were probably around eight and nine years old at the time. We sat them down and told them the story of a local family who was having a hard time. There were three children and the father was out of work. The mother was working some but with three small children, she wasn't able to do a lot.

They had bought a home and were two months behind on the payments. The bank had told them that they needed to catch up or the bank would foreclose and they would lose the house. No time is good to hear that sort of thing, but it seems even worse at Christmas. Not only could they not afford to buy presents for their children, they might not even be able to provide a house for them.

We asked our children if they would like to help this family. We also asked them how much money they were planning to spend on presents for us that year. Would it be all right to take that money and give it to the family to go toward their mortgage? We told them that we would take the money that we were planning to spend on presents for them and add it to the total amount. They didn't really understand until we told them that, by doing this, there would not be any presents under the tree for them from us. Both of them eagerly agreed to give the money and said they didn't need any presents.

After they were asleep that night we talked. Of course, since the children had been so sweet and loving, we wanted to go out and buy everything in sight to reward them. The only problem was that we couldn't do that. We felt it would cheapen their sacrifice as well as teach the wrong lesson.

Christmas Day got closer and closer. There were a few gifts from grandparents and relatives, but not many. They noticed that there was a lot of empty space under the tree. No one said anything else about presents.

We all got together to put cash in an envelope to mail anonymously to the family in need. We counted it and let the children know that it was enough to cover the back payments! We talked about how this family would be able to stay in their home for Christmas. We trusted God to look after the money and get it to the right place.

Christmas morning arrived. It didn't take long to open the few presents that were there but neither of our children complained. They did ask if we thought the family would need money again the next year and hoped that they wouldn't. It was also touching to hear them answer the questions from their friends about their presents and not say anything about their decision.

As parents, it is difficult to really know what impact our attempts at shaping our childrens' characters has had. However, in this case, we did get a glimpse. Many years later, while eavesdropping on a youth group, I heard the leader ask the young adults if they would tell about the best Christmas they could remember. Our daughter, Amy, put her hand up almost immediately and said; "It was the one when we were able to help a family keep their home." No details, just a quick glimpse of a lesson learned.

Celebrate God for our families!

*Beloved,
let us love one another:
for love is of God;
and every one that loveth
is born of God,
and knoweth God.*

1 John 4:7 (KJV)

Knock, Knock

t was the Christmas season and we were all getting into the spirit at work. There was a group planning our party, and during the planning session someone asked if there would be a needy family to sponsor this year. Each year, our department would get the name of a family in need and we would buy presents for them as well as the fixings for their Christmas dinner. It was great to see that the entire group wanted to continue this tradition.

We were given the name of a family with lots of children and the fun began. As the holiday got closer, the pile of presents got higher. There were enough of us to provide several presents for each of the children as well as for the parents. Each of the gifts was wrapped in fancy paper with ribbon and looked very festive. A day or so before Christmas Eve, we began to gather all of the food items we needed.

My good friend, Jeanna, and I were assigned the job of delivery. My daughter, Amy, joined us and after dark on Christmas Eve we went to "stake out" the family's home. We couldn't tell if they were home or not so we sat in the dark down the block in Jeanna's car to observe. It wouldn't do to leave a turkey and other fresh food sitting outside for any length of time. Soon a car pulled in the driveway and we watched the family pile out of the car and go into the house. They weren't carrying any presents or food that we could tell.

After a short while, we decided to deliver the presents. We had also decided that we did not want the family to know who had brought them, wanting it to be a total surprise. We each got out of the car, tiptoed up to the front door as quietly as we could, and left some presents. Then we returned to the car for another load and kept doing this until the car was empty and the doorway was overflowing. We felt a little like criminals trying to move with such stealth. With each trip, we hoped and prayed that no one would hear us and come to the door. Finally, all was delivered.

Then we worried that they might not come outside again until morning and if that happened, their meal would be ruined. Jeanna and I quietly returned to her car and left Amy standing by the door. She was young and a good runner, so the plan was for her to ring the doorbell and run back to the car before anyone could get to the door. She did just that. We watched from a distance as the father opened the door and saw all of the gifts. He called into the house and everyone piled out onto the front lawn to explore the treasures that were there. He looked up and down the street but we were in the car several houses away with the lights off and he couldn't see us.

What fun we had that night and what a blessing we received as we watched this family dance around and exclaim with joy at what they had found at their doorstep.

When God knocks at the door of our hearts, He doesn't run away like we did. He wants us to open the door and find Him there so that He can give us the best gift of all: eternity with Him! Won't you knock at His door so He can give you all that you need?

Celebrate God for His knock!

Ask your heavenly Father
for spiritual insights;
He'll give them to you.
Look for heavenly blessings
and you'll find them;
and when you knock on your heavenly
Father's door, He'll open
His whole storehouse for you.

Matthew 7:7 (The Clear Word)

One Nation

*A*round our country in November there are lots of parades and programs on Veteran's Day. It always brings tears to my eyes to see the proud veterans of World War II, sixty plus years later, standing tall in their uniforms. Many of them like to tell their war stories and to get together with members of their units from long ago. These Veterans' celebrations also bring sadness to my heart when I remember the reception given to many of the returning soldiers from Vietnam. Missing were the parades and the recognition for most of them. It is heartening to see that much has been done to try to change that.

This has a special meaning to me because I was there in Vietnam. Not as military personnel, but as a missionary. I saw many of the sights and visited with many of the servicemen. It was a life-changing experience for me. Prior to going to a country at war, I pretty much took our country for granted. The Pledge of Allegiance was something I said in a rote manner at ballgames without giving any thought to the words. Not so anymore!

While I was in Saigon, (Ho Chi Minh City)

Vietnam, there was much unrest and anti-American feeling. Jeeps and American flags were being burned, and anti-American slogans were everywhere.

The Vietnamese soldiers were supposed to be our allies, but many of them were involved in this anti-American activity and it was difficult to know where I was safe. I didn't have a car, so during that time there were occasions when I would take public transportation to different orphanages to return babies we had cared for at our mission hospital.

One of these orphanages was across the street from the American Embassy in Saigon. Traffic was beyond congested, there were people everywhere, and barbed-wire fencing and checkpoints were prominently located.

However, amidst the commotion and noise, whenever I looked up to the top of the Embassy Building I could see a large American flag. I never was able to look up at that beautiful red, white, and blue flag without a feeling of peace coming over me and without getting tears in my eyes. It was at those times that the Pledge of Allegiance became real to me. "One nation, under God..." Wow! That flag ceased to be a small, ordinary piece of fabric at those times.

My husband, Paul, was in the Army in Vietnam. During basic training, he was given a set of dog tags. Those dog tags are long gone, however, at a recent Veteran's Day ceremony, he received a new dog tag. This one has a picture of the flag on the front along with the words, "United States of America—One Nation Under

God." The reverse side says: "I will be strong and courageous. I will not be terrified, or discouraged; for the Lord my God is with me wherever I go. Joshua 1:9." Now that is a dog tag to keep and remember!

Celebrate God for our great country!

I've commanded you to be
strong and brave.
Don't ever be afraid or discouraged!
I am the Lord your God,
and I will be there
to help you wherever you go.
Joshua 1:9 (CEV)

Hurricane Charley

*W*hen Hurricane Charley hit our home in Port Charlotte, Florida, we were in Chicago. The day after the eye passed over our neighborhood, we drove as fast as we could to Florida to see if we still had a home and to assess the damage. On the trip down, we had no news whatsoever about our place. We later learned that power, water, and telephone services were all out. The cell towers were down so cell phones couldn't be used either. Since the trip from Chicago is about 1200 miles, we had a long time to think about and discuss what our situation might be.

On that drive, we noticed something unusual. There were long convoys of electrical trucks, tree removal trucks, and National Guard vehicles. As we passed them, the people would wave and give us encouraging signs that they were on the way to help our town. This lifted our spirits and made us even more proud of our wonderful country.

The news reports coming out of our area were pretty grim, but there was no way they could have prepared us for what we found. The destruction was described by some as being in a war zone.

Most of the trees were down. The power poles were snapped in half and the wires hung where they had fallen. Everywhere we looked houses were missing roofs, windows were shattered, and debris cluttered the area. It seemed that all of the familiar landmarks were gone. We have lived there for over 28 years and, even after all that time, we had difficulty finding our way around because nothing looked the same.

You may wonder how this situation would lend itself to celebrating God. Let me tell you how.

Neighbors helped neighbors. National Guardsmen directed traffic and kept order. Volunteer groups were set up everywhere passing out water and ice to everyone. The Red Cross drove down the streets offering a hot meal to all of those working on their homes or still assessing the damage in a state of panic and disbelief. During that first week "post-Charley" we didn't hear any harsh words or see any illegal activity. The main topics of conversation were the damage and the need for cleanup and repair, but there also were many conversations about being thankful that lives had been spared and that there were very few injuries.

My personal study of the Bible leads me to believe that time is short for this world. I believe that calamities will become more prevalent as prophesied in the Bible. I believe that God is present everywhere around us and that He wants desperately for us to take notice of Him and of His blessings to us. I believe that He is anxious to send His son, Jesus Christ, to take us home to Heaven to live with Him for eternity. He wants us to love Him and to love those around us just like He does. He doesn't want just a few; He wants everyone to be ready to go with Jesus when He returns to gather His children home. That includes you and me!

Celebrate God for the gift of His son, Jesus Christ!

For God so loved the world,
that he gave his only begotten Son,
that whosoever believeth in him
should not perish,
but have everlasting life.
John 3:16 (KJV)

Mission
Stories
from
Vietnam

Destination: Saigon

*D*o all children read mission stories and want to go overseas when they grow up? It seems like there were many of my peers, including me, that did. And all of us dreamed of going to Africa. That was the mission field as far as we knew. We saw pictures of natives with spears and war paint and thrilled with the thought that one day we might be able to make a difference in their lives. We knew, of course, that the only way to go to the mission field was to study and learn a profession that could be of use to the natives. So, with that in mind, I decided to be a nurse.

Years later, after finishing nursing school and graduate school, the time arrived to volunteer in the mission field. It was 1970, and our country was in turmoil. The thought of spending time in the great open spaces of Africa was very attractive. The church leaders asked me where I would like to go, and I must admit, that even though I always dreamed of Africa, I had no idea how big it was or how many countries were there. Not having any specific objective, my answer was, "Send me anywhere you need me. A place you can't get anyone else to go."

In short order, the "call" arrived. I was being asked to serve in Saigon, Vietnam! Vietnam, of all places. No way could I even find the country on a globe! Of course, I was very aware of the fact that we were in a war over there. Several of my friends and classmates had been invited by Uncle Sam to visit there, and not for the purpose of being missionaries, either. My parents were horrified and worried, my brother thought I was crazy to even consider it, and my friends had mixed and varied thoughts on the subject. It was tempting to ask, "Why not Africa?" but I had spent much time in prayer and asking the Lord to lead in my life. Was I now going to pretend that He messed up and made a mistake about the place I was to serve? Could I really hope to witness for Him if I was unwilling to go where I had been asked?

The assignment was to be the director of a School of Nursing in Saigon. The school was a three-year nursing program, just getting started. The first class had not yet finished the program and the curriculum was not yet fully developed. There was only one other teacher from the United States who had been there for a year. The former director was leaving immediately to return home. Some of the classes were being taught by Vietnamese nurses whose education was unclear. It is probably providential that I didn't even know enough to ask the right questions, because those answers could have kept me awake at night!

While continuing to ask for guidance from on High, I said yes to the call and began packing and preparing for a two year adventure like nothing I had ever experienced.

Some of my best friends assured me that, since I was leaving during my "prime dating years," I was sure to end up an "old maid." Others informed me that I would certainly lose ground professionally and be unable to find a good position when I returned to the United States.

Two years later, I returned home and had no difficulty obtaining a great job. Also, I have just celebrated my thirtieth wedding anniversary with a wonderful husband that I met; yes you guessed it, dressed in green fatigues in downtown Saigon.

When you ask God to be in charge of your life, He really is in charge. He knows what you need and when you need it. All you need to do is ask.

Celebrate God for opportunities to serve Him!

Jesus replied,
"Why do you say 'if you can?'
Anything is possible
for someone who has faith!"
Mark 9:23 (CEV)

Carpe Diem

rriving in Vietnam as a missionary had a very different orientation period than arriving there as a soldier. My husband tells me that when he arrived in Saigon as a Private in the Army, he quickly deplaned, all the time watching for the bunkers and other military presence. He had been briefed as to what to expect and was a little surprised to note that the sky in Vietnam was the same shade of blue as at home. Also the clouds were shaped just like the ones hovering over the United States. He arrived thinking of guns and bullets, and raced out of the plane, keeping the location of the closest bunker in mind.

My plane landed and, wide-eyed, I proceeded down the steps at the airport, mindless of the military presence surrounding the area. There were soldiers all around, and the sound of artillery could be heard. But what really caught my eye was all of the beautiful young girls lined up with a long banner that said, "Welcome Miss Gail." I took one look at their shining faces and immediately fell in love with them and their country. They were dressed in their student nurse uniforms and there was no doubt that they were my welcoming committee.

Meeting so many new people was quite overwhelming. The introductions were lengthy because the names were different and difficult for a novice to pronounce. However, soon after being introduced to all of the students, they began asking me when I would start teaching. They didn't want to miss any classes at all and wanted to learn everything they could, as fast as they could. Their desire was to start working as nurses and helping the sick people as soon as possible. They were very motivated!

Prior to going to Vietnam, I was teaching nursing in California. There were many great students there, also, who were anxious to be able to help the sick. However, in addition, there were students who were only in nursing because their parents wanted them to be nurses or they thought it would be good job security. One day after class, one of those students came up to me and asked, "What is the least I need to do to pass your class?" That question seemed a little strange to ask the teacher, but it was not terribly uncommon. You see, in our country, the students had many other options. In Vietnam, the nursing students knew that this was the only chance they had to get an education and better their lives.

Classes began the day after I arrived. Each day was packed with instruction and time at the hospital caring for patients. There were English classes that were taught by servicemen who volunteered their time; however, there were occasions when all of the bases were on alert and they were not allowed to travel to the mission compound.

On those occasions, the servicemen had no way to notify us, except by their absence. When this would happen, I could expect some of the students to track me down and say, "You will teach this class for us?" And I did.

At the hospital they were just as eager, not wanting to miss seeing and doing any procedures that needed to be done. They learned how to assess the patients and how to care for them. They also were very anxious to pass on what they learned to the new students. They couldn't wait to share their new knowledge. They were excited!

All of my life, I have been learning about Jesus and His great sacrifice for me. I have read His "textbook" and felt His presence near to me on many occasions. I have been excited about His working in my life. Why am I not as busy as those Vietnamese girls in sharing my knowledge?

Celebrate God for enthusiasm!

I am proud of the good news!
It is God's powerful way
of saving all people who have faith,
whether they are Jews or Gentiles.
Romans 1:16 (CEV)

Anywhere
With Jesus

*A*nywhere with Jesus I can safely go, Anywhere He leads me in this world below, Anywhere without Him dearest joys would fade, Anywhere with Jesus I am not afraid." Do you recognize that song from the hymnal?

It is no surprise that this became the theme song for the missionaries living in Saigon, Vietnam, in the early 70's. Being one of them, let me give you a few examples of why this song had so much meaning for us.

One morning at our church service, we noticed that one of the doctors and his wife had not come. Thinking that they were late or perhaps just too tired to attend, we proceeded with the service. The mission compound was not very large and after the service, some of the missionaries went to the doctor's home to check on him. They found the doctor and his wife tied up and gagged. Several of their belongings had been stolen, but they were alive and safe.

Another time, word came to the compound that

there was a man outside the wall that was bleeding. He was found and brought in for treatment. His injury was actually the amputation of his hands and the reason given was that he had assisted the Americans. For that crime, his hands were cut off by the Viet Cong. Now he could not continue to help the Americans. He would also be an example to other Vietnamese that helping Americans was not tolerated.

Inside the wall surrounding the mission compound was the School of Nursing, an elementary school, a Serviceman's Center, and housing for the nursing students and missionaries. What was not inside the compound was the mission hospital. It was one mile away through very busy streets. The nursing students worked in the hospital for their practical experience and as their teacher, I needed to be there. The mission had only one car and it was not mine; I walked the mile to and from the hospital each day. One mile is not far, but it can be difficult when all of the streets are crowded with people, bicycles, motorcycles, cars, and military vehicles.

One day, while on the way to the hospital and dressed in my nursing uniform, a military truck full of RVN (Republic of Vietnam) soldiers drove by, showering me with pieces of broken glass. At that time there was a lot of anti-American feelings. I had foolishly thought that being in my uniform would let them know that I was only there to help their people. The uniform didn't help; being an American was enough to make them want to hurt me.

Another day on the same route, dressed in the same

nursing uniform, three young men jumped from behind a wall and started hitting me. I am 5' 11" tall barefoot with my hair wet, and the tallest Vietnamese I ever met came to my shoulder. This was good because I was able to get away from them and run.

At the hospital there were days when I was the only American on the grounds. On a few occasions while working there, one of the men from the office would come and get me. He would take me to an old truck and tell me to get in and cover myself up with blankets, then he would drive out of the hospital area quickly. The reason for all of this was that the Vietnamese soldiers were burning anything that was American. Just having an American on the premises made it unsafe for the hospital.

Because of these examples, you can see why we were drawn to the song. We sang it at every service and prayed for God's guidance and protection. Our song services were always rousing and especially so when arriving at the chorus: "Anywhere, anywhere, fear I cannot know. Anywhere with Jesus I can safely go."

Celebrate God for His protection!

*I will be with you always,
even until the end of the world.*

Matthew 28:20 (CEV)

Best In Class

*D*on't you feel good when you know you are the best? That was how we felt in Saigon, Vietnam. Our mission hospital was recognized as the best in the city, not only by the local people but also by the local government officials! It was only supposed to hold 38 patients, but the census was almost never below the middle seventies. There were patients lining all of the hallways and, if an office door could be opened during the night, a litter would routinely be slipped into that space. Patients' family members would vie with other families to crowd their loved ones into any and all possible spaces.

Our hospital was the only one in the city that provided nursing care 24 hours a day. It was really the only one that provided nursing care at all. In the hospitals that we visited around town, the nurses worked from eight to five and then left the patients to the care of their families. If no family was available, no care was provided. Even when the nurses were there, it was difficult to see care being given. One hospital had running water for the patients and families but for only one or two hours a day, so personal hygiene was virtually nonexistent.

Another hospital paid its staff for the job, not the hours. One day while the students and I were at that hospital, one of the nurses started her day early and by ten o'clock she was off to spend the rest of the day with her boyfriend. The problem was that she was the medicine nurse and between 6:00 a.m. and when she left at 10:00 a.m., she gave all of the medicine, some ordered for once a day, some twice a day, and some four times a day. It was all given at once and off she went knowing that she would be paid for the whole day because all of the medicine was given.

For many of the patients, food was brought in by their families. There was no evidence of any provision for special diets for diabetics, or any other patients with certain conditions. In some hospitals, a large rolling tray table would arrive on the unit and the families or patients themselves would go to the tray and get whatever they could find. And, of course, no record was made of who was eating what.

At our hospital, personal care was given to all of the patients, food was provided and an effort was made to give each patient the food that best suited his/her needs as well as their tastes. Nurses were on the wards around the clock and medications were dispensed at the times ordered as well as documentation made on the patient's record.

As I said, our hospital was considered the best. However, it seems necessary to ask the question, "Is the best an absolute or relative term?" Our hospital was an old French villa that had been remodeled into a hospital. There were three floors and no elevator, just a circular, winding staircase. Try to imagine moving patients up and down that staircase on litters! It was quite tricky not to tip them off the bottom of their litter. It was also quite tricky to make the trip with intravenous bottles and other equipment attached to the patient.

In a small room on the second floor there was a very large pot. It sat on a burner of sorts and all of the reusable supplies were boiled in that pot. There was no way to measure heat but the staff did try to keep track of how long the items boiled.

Linen was another problem. As you can imagine, there was no modern laundry connected to the hospital. The sheets and other linens were taken to the mission compound a mile away, and washed, then hung out on the line to dry. Not too bad in the dry season, but a real challenge in the rainy season!

The Vietnamese people are excellent at adapting and seemed to always come up with solutions to problems. One of my favorites was the oxygen supply. There was a large green cylinder on the ground floor that serviced the Emergency Room. This cylinder also had to take care of any patients on the second or third floor. Fortunately, not too many patients needed it, but when they did, the resourceful staff connected IV tubing, one after another, and strung it on the handrail of the winding staircase up to the higher floors. There it was attached to Y-connectors and more IV tubing as necessary.

Is being the best absolute or relative? Probably most would say relative in the case of our little hospital. It was definitely the best available there at that time. However, it certainly had many issues that would probably not be acceptable to most of us here and now. Isn't it great that we do not have to make that sort of decision when considering our life and our walk with Jesus? There is nothing relative about that, it is definitely the absolute BEST there is!

Celebrate God for creativity!

*But my God shall supply
all your need according to his riches
in glory by Christ Jesus.*

Philippians 4:19 (KJV)

Mission: Possible

It's nice to have a job that is a challenge. But what about a job that is impossible? One person can only be in so many places and do so many things at one time. If the job requires more, what then? These were questions that I asked myself after arriving in Saigon, Vietnam, to be the Director of a School of Nursing.

The school was in its second year of operation and had thirty students attending. The third year had not been planned, no lessons prepared, and it would soon be time to interview and select the twenty-five young women to begin as first-year students. The previous director left for the U.S. as soon as I arrived, so there was no orientation period. There I was with students to teach, labs to supervise, lesson plans to do, third-year curriculum to develop, and new students to interview. I also needed to interact with the government officials to get the program recognized and to open up opportunities for clinical experience in different hospital and community settings.

That was work! There was also the challenge of a new culture, new language, and a new environment. Even the electricity didn't work like it did at home. Soon after arriving, I washed my hair, rolled it, and set out to dry it with my hair dryer. At that time, my hair was long and very thick. After about twenty minutes under the little hood of the hair dryer there was a burning smell and the dryer motor decided it was done. It was the rainy season and very damp, and my hair was still very wet. Because of the way it rains, you are always wet. After my hair had remained damp for 2 weeks, I was afraid it would grow mildew, so I had it all cut off.

It was important to me to try to learn the language. I told the students that if we were discussing a patient, we would do that in English with a translator, but for any other communication, they were only to respond in Vietnamese. Did they ever take me at my word! Immediately my social conversation came to a standstill. Since the language is tonal, there are multiple ways to pronounce each word and each pronunciation has a different meaning. For example, one day at the hospital, I went to the window and thought I was saying, "It is raining." When the students rushed over to try to help me, I discovered that what I had said was, "I am going to vomit." Communication was difficult at best, but the students stuck to it and forced me to struggle to speak in their language. We laughed a lot at my attempts!

Before leaving America, all of my belongings were shipped by boat. I was assured that sending the goods six weeks before leaving would ensure that everything would be there when I arrived. Upon my arrival in Saigon I stepped off the plane with one suitcase that weighed only 17 pounds. Traveling light seemed like a good idea since all of my things would be waiting for me. Right? Wrong! Not only were my things not there, they did not arrive for over 3 months! During that time, my wardrobe consisted of one uniform, one dress, and very little else.

So as a new missionary in Vietnam, I no longer had the hairstyle or the appliances I was used to. Neither did I have the clothes I had planned on wearing, my old friends to hang out with, or the food I was accustomed to eating. Added to all these changes, I had a job that was overwhelming and challenging, to say the least.

Prior to this adventure, I was very self-sufficient. If there was something I needed or wanted, I would set out to get it and do just that in most cases. I acknowledged God's presence but didn't really feel the need of His help in most projects. My life ran along smoothly and my prayer life was filled largely with cliches and repetition. Not so anymore. To wake up each day knowing that I had no clue how to get things done or who to turn to, it became natural to just turn it all over to God and try to follow His leading. In short order, He taught me that He really was there and cared about who I was and what I was trying to do. For me, it took an overwhelming challenge to learn to depend on Him, but it doesn't need to be that way. He really wants to be there

for all of us and is only waiting for the invitation.
Celebrate God for challenges!

*I'm in despair
and far from home.
My heart is faint
and my courage is gone.
Lead me to a place of safety,
to the Rock
that is higher than I.*

Psalm 61:2 (The Clear Word)

A Saigon Christmas

*W*hen you think of Christmas, do you think of decorated pine trees? I do! I love those beautiful trees, full of multicolored lights and ornaments. There are always at least five strings of lights on our tree and the rest of the space is taken up with handmade ornaments that my husband's mother and sisters crafted for us. The first Christmas we were married, we received a box loaded with sequined, sewn, or painted ornaments, and every year since then they have added to our collection with new and different decorations. We also have ceramic and cross stitch ones. Our tree is so beautiful all dressed up in it's finery.

There was a year, however, when my tree was different. That year was my first Christmas in Saigon, Vietnam. The holiday season was fast approaching and there was nowhere to get a tree. There were very few trees left in the crowded city and none of them were of the Christmas variety. There were no stores even to buy an artificial one, so it was hard to get into the spirit of Christmas. One day, a box arrived in the mail from my parents. They had sent some presents and goodies, and then added one string of Christmas lights. Having the lights made the absence of a tree even worse.

About that time, a young man who was working in the Central Highlands came through our mission. He stayed for a few days, heard us wishing for a tree, and then left. A week or so later, a big truck pulled up to our mission. A man got off, unloaded a tree with a little note on it that said, "For Gail," and drove off. What a tree! It had been cut and bound with rope for the trip and, because of curfews and roadblocks, it had taken a lot longer than anticipated for the transportation. There had not been a way to keep it in water for the trip. Try to imagine a tree about six feet tall with very sparse branches to begin with, but that now had several of those broken and bent. In addition, the needles, once green, were now mostly brown and rapidly falling off. It sounds pretty sad, but to us it was beautiful!

We put our single string of lights on it and began making ornaments. We attempted to string popcorn, which is a lot harder to do than it looks, and made paper chains. It wasn't very fancy, but it was our tree and we had it because of the effort of one young man who went out of his way to make our holiday a little better. He had thought of us and taken the time to find a tree and arrange for it to be brought to us. When we looked at the tree, we didn't really notice how out of shape it was or even the little piles of brown needles on the floor; we saw him and his act of love to us.

Celebrate God for thoughtful acts!

And it shall come to pass,
that before they call,
I will answer;
and while they are yet speaking,
I will hear.

Isaiah 65:24 (KJV)

Travel Orders

*W*herever there is a war, there are servicemen. Have you ever wondered what they do when they are off duty or what they think about when out of the line of fire? Being in Saigon during the war gave me an opportunity to see and hear some of the answers to those questions.

At the mission compound there was a Serviceman's Center with a civilian chaplain. When soldiers had time off or were able to sign out for a day or a weekend, they were encouraged to come to the Center. There they could visit with the missionaries, eat home cooked meals, play games, and sleep in clean sheets without worrying about anything. Lots of the servicemen took advantage of the facility and got to know something about the mission work there. Some of these men volunteered to help teach English to the students, and some helped with construction and work around the compound. It gave them a home away from home to feel part of.

Occasionally, letters would come to the mission from parents back home. The usual message was to ask if we had seen or heard from their son. It seemed that some young men saw the military as a way to escape and get away from all of the pressures at home, including their religious upbringings. Whenever possible we would try to find the young man and invite him to the Center. The search, many times, led us to other parts of the country.

One weekend, just prior to the Christmas holidays, one such letter arrived. Upon checking, we discovered that this particular GI was supposed to be stationed in Hue, very close to the DMZ (demilitarized zone). The student missionary and I flew out of Saigon on a C-130 in search of him. At the base in Hue, we ran into a dead-end and were never able to contact this young man. However, we were there and our transport back to Saigon was not leaving until the next day. We decided to look for another soldier or two that might need someone to talk with them.

After dinner, there was a party scheduled that many of the fellows were planning to attend. Their main objective, they said, was to get drunk and forget the war. It didn't sound like a party that we wanted to attend! After getting multiple invitations from them, we said that we were going to the chapel to sing Christmas carols and invited them to join us. Off we went to the chapel. Neither one of us could be considered a great singer, so the first few songs could only be described as rough. We labored through just one or two carols before some of the fellows started to arrive. As each new voice was added to our "choir," it sounded better and better.

For over four hours we sang, and by the end of that

time, there weren't any empty seats in the chapel. Officers and enlisted men alike were there singing with all their hearts about the birth of our Savior. We were all pretty hoarse, but also very happy, as we closed up the chapel that night.

A few of the men stayed behind to walk us to our quarters, but they really just needed to talk. One officer told me that he had just about given up his faith after all he had experienced in the war. He then said that hearing those songs about Jesus had awakened memories in him. He was going to go back to his barracks that night and write to his wife about all that had happened to him, and beg her forgiveness for forgetting how God was in charge of everything. No one preached that night and if they had, the seats probably would not have been full. But the presence of the Savior was there, and He was busily showering His children with feelings of love and peace.

In the morning there was a lot of fog. Our plane was scheduled to leave at 0800 hours and we needed to be at the airport well before that to be assured of a seat on the transport. We got up early and looked out the window realizing there was no way we were going to be able to leave the base in time. Because of the fog, the minesweepers had not been able to clear the road and driving before that was done was considered suicide. We waited anxiously and finally were told that it was safe to go to the airport, well past the scheduled time of departure. Even though we were sure that we had missed our flight and knew that no other planes were scheduled that day, we went anyway just to check.

Arriving at the airport, we saw that the plane was still there. We couldn't believe it! We went up to the officer in charge and asked if we could still get aboard. He told us that the plane had been ready to leave for some time but that it was being held for two VIPs. We were so thankful that some others had not been able to get there in time either and hurriedly raced out to board the plane. As soon as we were in, the door was closed and the plane took off. We asked the co-pilot what happened to the VIPs? To which he replied, "You are the VIPs."

God had our whole trip planned for us. We weren't able to accomplish our objective of finding that one soldier, but obviously that wasn't God's plan. He wanted us there for a different reason, and He arranged for all of the pieces to be in place to accomplish His plan.

Celebrate God for His plans for us!

*For as the heavens are higher
than the earth, so are my ways
higher than your ways,
and my thoughts than your thoughts.*

Isaiah 55:9 (KJV)

Weapon of Mercy

At the mission in Saigon, there was a student missionary whose job it was to schedule and conduct immunization clinics for the children. These clinics would last three to four hours each, and could be several hours away from the city. Multiple immunizations were administered, including tetanus, typhoid, and cholera. To administer the vaccine, a gun was used. The child's arm would be held firmly in one hand while the gun was snuggled up tightly to the arm with the other hand. It was a very efficient method of giving the shots because the children could be lined up, the shot given, the gun end disinfected, and the next child immunized. Very fast and usually painless.

One day, the clinic was scheduled to be held down South in the delta. It required traveling by a canoe on one of the tributaries of the Mekong River into an area not visited by many foreigners. The student missionary and I were scheduled to do this clinic. We gathered up all of the gear and left early in the morning to take the ride down river. At times, the river was very narrow and we could look up at the banks and see soldiers patrolling with their guns. Our guides requested that we sit or lie down as low as possible in the canoe so as not to be observed by the soldiers. This worked most of the time but there were a few shots fired in our direction during the trip anyway. A canoe is not very big when you are crouched over and surrounded by medical equipment. It was a long trip!

After several hours, we arrived at a small village. The people there were very curious and often would come up to us and touch our hair or "pet" our arms. Later we learned that there had never been an American in this village before, much less American females. While we set up the area for the clinic, we had quite an audience. No work happened in the village that day because all of the villagers, men, women, and children, were there to observe what was done. In due time, the clinic was ready to begin. Our guides translated for us and helped form the children into lines so we could begin. The children were great and after the first few went through the line, there was a lot of laughter and playing for the remainder of the clinic.

When all of the children had been immunized, the villagers insisted that we stay long enough to share a meal with them before leaving. We were able, through our translators, to help them understand the reason for the shots and also some very basic public health principles to be used in their homes.

Our goal was to provide protection to these children from the diseases that were all around them, and to help their families understand about health, Divine guidance, and how it all related to their happiness and fullness of life. The medicine gave us an opening to meet these villagers and to share our faith!

Celebrate God for modern medicine!

> *The Lord God is waiting*
> *to show how kind he is*
> *and to have pity on you.*
> *The Lord always does right;*
> *he blesses those who trust him.*
>
> *Isaiah 30:18 (CEV)*

About the Author

Gail Pelley is a Registered Nurse, wife, and mother of two adult children. She draws on her personal experiences in each of these areas for the stories in this book. A strong belief in God and His blessings, as well as a desire to help others see the workings of God in their lives, has led her to write this book. All of these stories come directly from actual events in her life.